Praise for Helen Astin's
The Road from Serres

"A completely readable and well-constructed account of a young girl's journey from German-occupied Greece in WWII to academic prominence in the U.S. A testament to human spirit, and an inspiration for all feminists. Very enjoyable."

ENGIN INEL HOLMSTROM, PhD,
Sociologist and Author of *Loveswept*

"Lena Astin gives us a revealing memoir that takes us from her childhood in Greece to her retirement in Malibu. I expected a story of how she became a feminist, but from her accounts of her independent spirit even as a young girl, it seems she was born one!"

CAROL TAVRIS,
Social Psychologist and Writer

"As a feminist foremother in the fields of psychology and higher education, Lena Astin has been an inspiration and mentor to countless students and colleagues. This engaging memoir tells us how she pursued her passions, her career, and her life as wife and mother."

ANNE PEPLAU,
Distinguished Research Professor
of Psychology, UCLA

"Those of you fortunate enough to have known Lena and her ground breaking research on women will once again experience her authenticity and wisdom in this candid memoir. Those of you who have not been so fortunate will find an absorbing story of a courageous émigré from World War II Greece, who contributes mightily to her adopted country. Thank you, Lena, for taking me into all the richness of your adventurous life."

—ART CHICKERING,
Pitkin Fellow, Goddard College, Plainfield, VT

"Reading Helen Astin's memoir is to be taken in a wondrous sweep of a deeply lived life. The smell of Greek lilacs, jasmine, olive trees, and the Aegean follow Lena wherever she lives. We meet her first as a little girl with a white bow in her hair who later grows into a woman determined to achieve her dreams. She throws open the doors of her life and invites us in as friends. Narrated with stories that are funny, serious, self-deprecating, and at times brutally honest, we are touched by her grace and beauty. From early rough and tumble days working in a federal penitentiary to the halls of academe, Lena reminds us that relationships are everything. Loving and respectful family bonds that reach from Greece to California, like her enduring friendships, form this remarkable woman, and remind us of what is important in life."

—WELLFORD WILMS
Author and Professor in the Educational Leadership
Program at UCLA's Graduate School of Education
and Information Studies

The Road from Serres

The Road from Serres

A Feminist Odyssey

BY HELEN STAVRIDOU ASTIN

Printed in the United States of America.

Designed by Backstory Design
Set in 11.25 point Goudy by Marcovaldo Productions, Inc.

Cataloging-in-Publication data for this book is available from the
Library of Congress.
First edition 2014
ISBN: 978-0-9905489-1-1 (Paperback)
ISBN: 978-0-9905489-2-8 (eBook)

10 9 8 7 6 5 4 3 2 1

To my beloved granddaughters
Erin, Amalia, and Ila

CONTENTS

CONTENTS

Prelude

It is March 1998, and I am flying back from a challenging and invigorating two-and-a-half-day conference back east about "Women and Leadership." The conference theme was on how to develop women's leadership potential with a focus on the ethical basis of leadership, responsibility, collaboration, and social action. I pick up the February issue of *Time* magazine for some airplane reading. The Cinema section catches my attention because of its title and subtitle: "Hard Rites of Passage: A Flock of European Films Depict Childhood Ordeals." The title itself sends me back to my own childhood in occupied Greece during the Second World War. Flashes of past memories pass through my mind's eye: bombs falling while I am hiding behind a chair; people dying in the streets from famine; Jews being taken away to concentration camps; freezing bedrooms; studying at night by kerosene lamp; dreaming of being a pianist; sleeping on the dining room table; fantasies of having a beautiful home where I can bring friends for sleepovers.

I open the magazine hurriedly, eager to read the article with reviews of recent European movies, hoping to find myself in those stories. To my amazement, all the stories are written by men and depict the experiences of young boys. Where is my voice? How are we going to achieve gender equality without a better understanding and appreciation of all peoples: women's experiences, men's experiences, the experiences of blacks and Latinos? I momentarily despair, but quickly I vow to continue my commitment toward creating a more just society in every way I can.

– * –

For years now my youngest son Paul has been asking me to write my life's story. Having lived himself in Greece for over a year, being fluent in Greek and very interested in his Greek ancestry, he feels strongly that I owe it to my family to do so. It is a must as a gift for my granddaughters, he says. So I made a promise to myself to share with them stories of my life by writing my memoirs after I retire.

About two years ago, I was invited by UCLA's Center for the Study of Women, in collaboration with the Library's Center for Oral History Research at UCLA, to participate in an oral history project about my life and work on behalf of women nationally and at UCLA. I readily accepted their invitation. I saw it as an opportunity to begin the process of writing about my life—the promise I made to myself and to my son. My retirement took place in 2010 at the completion and publication of my last academic book. Two years after that, as I turned eighty years of age, I embarked on the writing of my memoir.

I've found that recounting my life in writing, with all its pleasures and pains, was like holding a mirror in front of me. I got to know myself a lot better. Writing my life's story enabled me to go more deeply into my past. Some memories came to me readily. For other events I had to dig deeply inside to see myself in a more intimate way, tasting the highs of my career and family and the lows of my life's journey: the war years, the deaths, the famine, and the family dislocation.

This memoir is written as a gift to my friends, colleagues, and former students who might be interested in knowing about my life in Greece during the war years, my immigrating in my late teens to this country, and my work as an academic feminist.

But most of all, it is a gift to my beloved family: my husband Sandy, my sons John and Paul. And, as I promised Paul, for my granddaughters Erin, Amalia, and Ila.

The Road from Serres

CHAPTER 1

Growing Up in Greece

February 6, 1932 is the day I was born, in Serres, a small town in northern Greece—a typical small town with all its charm and ease of getting around. My father, a civil engineer, held a high position in the public sector. We lived on the second floor of a two-storied house he had designed and built. It was surrounded by three gardens. To this day, the smell of Greek jasmine takes me back to that place. My Greek friend Kiki brought me some jasmine from Greece, which I planted in my backyard here in Los Angeles. The small jasmine cutting from Greece is now a huge bush—a constant reminder of my Greek heritage, and my first eight years growing up in Serres. This year I planted an olive tree outside my kitchen window as another reminder of my beloved country. My appreciation for the beauty in my surroundings comes from growing up in the house in Serres. Thinking of my early years there brings back memories of beautiful gardens filled with the delicious smell of honeysuckle, wisteria, and jasmine. My granddaughters tease me about how much I enjoy fixing up the house and arranging flowers, a very important part of my life and surroundings.

– * –

My parents' bedroom was large, with a veranda on two of its sides. Lilac wisteria climbed up the walls circling the Grecian balcony columns. All three gardens at the house were enclosed by a sculpted iron gate: a large flower garden and two elevated ones, reachable only by stairs. We had a strawberry patch, fruit trees, and plenty of vegetables.

The inside of the house was equally inviting. There was a salon decorated in deep red velvet—a room that remained closed unless we had special guests. I loved this room for its formality. It was mysterious but not cozy like the family room where we spent most of our time. In the family room, there was an old striped kilim rug in bold colors: black, red, yellow, and green. The couch and armchairs were a soft brick color. My mother had a favorite armchair, a comfortable brown leather chair with wooden armrests. It was placed next to the somba (a type of fireplace).

That chair has its own story about the war and about our having been displaced from Serres. Once we left Serres, in 1940, the Bulgarians, who were in alliance with the Germans and Italians, moved into our house. No one knows how my mother's chair plus a buffet ended up in an acquaintance's house in Salonica. While my mother was visiting there, years later, she found herself sitting in her own chair, the one from the house in Serres. She knew that it was hers because over the years, when she sat in it, she used to play with her toothpick, which made a small hole on the right arm of the chair. And that small hole gave it away. The new owners were happy to find the previous owner of the chair and the buffet, and they graciously returned them to my mother.

In our house in Serres, the dining table was placed close to the kitchen in the family room where we spent our time as a family—my brother and I playing on the floor, doing our homework at the table, or curling up on the couch. Alex's usual playtime activity was to set up his soldiers and military equipment, a favorite game of many young boys. And, for me, it was dolls and dollhouses. A chicken coop in the back of the house provided us with daily fresh eggs. Every afternoon, my mother would fix up our favorite afternoon snack. She would beat up a fresh egg with lots of sugar and cocoa—it was a delicious afternoon delight—an equivalent of today's frozen yogurt snack.

To the right of our house, two doors down, was a private clinic run by Dr. Makris, a family doctor who took care of everything, including performing surgeries. I loved seeing him leave the clinic to make house visits atop his white horse, looking distinguished with his wire-rimmed glasses and grey goatee. One day I asked Dr. Makris if I could watch an operation. Intrigued by my curiosity, he invited me to do so, and, soon enough, there I was, seven years old and watching an appendectomy. I was completely intrigued, watching the whole procedure with great fascination. I was not afraid or turned off by the sight of blood or the intestines sticking out of the patient's abdomen. In spite of my early fascination with medicine and the human body, I did not follow up on this early interest to become a medical doctor. Alex, my brother, is the one who pursued the medical profession while I went on to become an academic psychologist. Apocrypha has it that, as a young boy, Alex went to the clinic to observe an operation as well, nearly fainting at the sight of blood.

As the only girl in a neighborhood full of little boys, I learned to play all sorts of outdoor games. Though I was a good sport about participating, I never really enjoyed it. Quite often what I wanted to do was to play instead with my dolls and dollhouse. Lucky for me, Laki, the boy who lived next door, loved playing dolls with me. From time to time, I would invite him to come upstairs and play with me and my dolls. I have not seen Laki since then and I have often wondered what might have become of him.

By fall 1937, all the older kids from the neighborhood were in school except me; I was too young. I felt so alone without my playmates that I decided to walk to school and wait for them to come out. As I walked there that fall morning, the streets were empty. I passed a vast field, walked through the school playground, and sat on the school steps waiting for Alex, Lakis, Yannis, and Petros. After a couple of hours without seeing anyone coming out, I took myself back home, sad to be all alone again until the late afternoon when the kids returned.

When my father came home, my mother reported to him my school visit adventure. My father right away decided that I was ready to start school. But to do so, he needed to change my birth certificate to make me a year older and eligible for school. Given his position in the local government, he had the connections to make the change, and all of a sudden a new birth certificate appeared with a new birthdate, February 6, 1931. I was all excited that I could be with my buddies again. However, that seemingly simple act of changing a single digit on a date has haunted me over the years. In some important documents, I am listed as being born in 1931—Social Security, naturalization papers, driver's license—and in others, the year of birth is 1932. It is even more complicated than that, since when I left Greece I had no birth certificate, and only a few years ago I managed to get one that had the correct birth date. Unfortunately, the birth certificate is written in Greek, which creates its own translation issues whenever I am asked for it on special occasions.

I always loved school, and was always an excellent student. And while I wasn't always an easy child at home, I was the perfect child at school. At home I was a stubborn kid. When my mother would ask me something, I would tell her "no" before she even finished her sentence. I was sweet and easy with others, but not so with my parents. When my mother came to visit me in the U.S., I remember her looking at me and saying, "My God, I never thought you would turn out to be so good. You're a sweet woman now." My brother, as a child, never acted out at home as I did. He was obedient. Sometimes firstborns are like that, and my mother would often compare me to him, emphasizing how good he was and asking why I couldn't be more like him. That did not make me feel good or behave any better.

Growing up, I felt very close to my brother Alex, who is three and a half years older than me. As young children, we shared a bedroom. My parents had promised me that in a couple of years, my father would give me his study as "a room of my own." As an eight-year-old, I fantasized about how I would fix up the space to make it mine. That dream never materialized. It came to a halt when the war broke out in 1940.

− * −

When we lived in Serres, my grandparents lived not far from us. Every Sunday after church, we'd visit my grandparents, and my grandmother would have a wonderful spread of food. It was a sweet life. We had no concerns or pressures, and we were surrounded by love and family. As I think back, I feel that I was fortunate to experience my first eight years in that way, given all the hardships that came later on with the war.

As an eight-year-old, I didn't understand the significance of war. I didn't know what to expect. Americans had easy access to telephones and movies, but I grew up without any of these modern conveniences. We had a radio and that was it. We didn't have a car back then either.

The way I grew up in Greece seems similar to the generation of my husband's mother in this country, in terms of experiences and material goods. The two main activities were going to school and playing in the neighborhood to entertain ourselves. When we went out, we mainly did so with our parents and relatives. On Sunday, we'd go either to my grandmother's or to a nice place to have lunch and listen to music. In many ways, I lived a highly protected life, which made the transition from an easy and wonderful childhood to one full of fear, with limited living space and scarce food, a difficult one.

The Early Years of the War (1939-1941)

In 1939, when I was seven, rumors began circulating around the country that we were going to have a war. My grandfather decided that, for protection, it would be a good idea for all of the women and children in the family to move to a small village in middle Greece called Agrafa, where he was born and raised. There, five of us lived in a small house: Aunt Liberty, my mother's younger sister; her son Costas, who was two years old at the time; and my mother, Alex, and I. Often, we had field visitors, small mice that ran around like toys on wheels, to the amazement and delight of Costas. I didn't like them at all, not then and not now.

One fall afternoon the five of us decided to explore the village, some on horses and myself on a mule. That excursion turned from a fine idea into a nightmare for me. As we were moving through the streets of the village, my mule decided to go forward on his own, just like a mule. He took a sharp turn, away from the rest of the group. And there I was, all alone in a village I hardly knew. I had no idea where I was. I was scared, wondering where the house was or whether I would ever be able to reconnect with the rest of the group. Fortunately, he took another sharp turn and I saw the rest of the family. This episode has remained with me ever since, and to this day, I refuse to get up on a horse. Or a mule.

We spent less than a year in Agrafa before deciding to come back to Serres, since nothing was really happening around us as yet. Nonetheless, we knew that the war was going to hit Greece in the near future, given what was already happening in the rest of Europe. And sure enough, on October 28, 1940, the Italians invaded Greece. Greece decided that it was not going to give up without a fight. October 28 has since been declared a national holiday. It is called Ochi Day, which means "No, we're not going to surrender, we're going to fight."

My father, being well read and fluent in German, understood the German mentality and decided that the women and children in our family should go to Athens because the Germans, out of respect for the Acropolis and for what Athens stood for, would not bombard Athens. He was right; the Germans did not bomb Athens. In the meantime, the men of the family (my father and uncles) were called into the army and sent to different parts of the country. My father, being a civil engineer, got a desk job in Salonica. My uncles were sent to the border of Albania to protect Greece from further invasions.

The day we were to move from Serres to Athens came shortly after Ochi Day. My mother gave my brother and me a suitcase and told us to pack whatever we could, announcing that we were leaving the next day for Athens. I remember becoming confused, and all I could say, melodramatically, was: "But mama, how can I? I can't even fit my doll in this suitcase and I have a piano lesson next Tuesday." I had just started piano lessons. But as calm as she could be, she told us that this was it, and that was what we had to do. We left everything behind, all of our household belongings, and moved to Athens with one small suitcase each.

Greece was occupied soon after the Second World War began. Following the Italian invasion, the Germans occupied Greece in April 1941, and remained until October 1944. In Athens, my brother, my mother, and I lived in one room as renters in someone else's home. We went from a beautiful, spacious home in Serres to living all three of us in one room. Aunt Liberty and Cousin Costas rented a second room in the same house.

Life during the occupation brings back memories of limited quarters and not having enough food. One lovely Athenian evening I went to a classmate's house to visit with her and another friend, all of us students at the Berzan School, a private school run by a Frenchman, Mr. Berzan. My friend lived in a large apartment in a turn-of-the-century building. Every room was large, especially the kitchen. I looked with envy at that tastefully decorated apartment with its large dark pieces of furniture, so different from the one room where we lived on 1 Pippinou Street! As soon as I arrived at my friend's apartment, we went into the kitchen, took a piece of cheese out of the fridge, sat around the table, cut the piece of cheese, not more than two ounces, into three equal pieces, and put each piece on the scale to make sure that it was equally divided among the three of us.

Starvation was rampant in Greece. It has been estimated that over 300,000 civilians died in Athens alone from starvation during the first two years of the occupation. The Germans had availed themselves of most of the food. On many occasions Alex and I would go to the soup kitchens and wait in line for just a bit of food: some soup which was totally tasteless, a couple of potatoes, and one tomato.

After a year and a half of living in Athens, we decided to return back north to Salonica and rejoin my father. We traveled by train. At one of the stops, we got out and were quickly surrounded by Italian and German soldiers. It was lunchtime. I moved close to an Italian soldier who was eating his pasta. Oh, how I craved it. I stood near him, staring at him and his food like a hungry dog waiting to grab what was left from his master's dish. Here I was, a cute little girl with a huge white bow in her hair. The Italian soldier took one look at me and generously handed me his dish of pasta. Just as I started to eat, a German soldier approached us and grabbed it from me. As he handed it back to the Italian soldier, he began to reprimand him loudly for offering his lunch to the "enemy." This was one of many encounters I had with Germans that instilled such fear in me.

If I were out walking, the minute I heard German soldiers' boots behind me I'd begin to sweat with the strong fear of what might be next. And there was a next. One unforgettable night, it must have been around midnight, we heard a hard knock at the door. My mother opened the door and there stood two Germans with grim faces asking for the men in the house. My father and Alex came out of their room in their pajamas. The Germans ordered them to get dressed. "Come with us," they said. My mother and I put our coats over our nighties and followed the four of them as fast as we could, all of us walking in the middle of the night in silence. We arrived at some kind of an office building. My mother and I were sent back home while Alex and my father were taken into the building. No words were exchanged so none of us knew what this was all about. We walked back home wondering what would become of them—if we'd ever see them again, or if they'd end up tortured or killed. We had heard that for every German killed, one hundred Greeks would be killed in retaliation. I prayed that that would not be the fate for my father and brother. Thank God, the next day they were released unharmed. When they got back to the house, they said that they had been held without any explanation. To this day, I do not know what that was about other than perhaps a scare tactic.

While in Athens, we experienced many air raids, day and night. One day, as we were returning home from school, the sirens went off. People started to run in every possible direction, looking for the closest shelter. I looked around, frightened. All I wanted was to get home as fast as possible. Soon after I got home, everything went quiet again and life returned back to normal, but I couldn't help but still feel great apprehension about what was happening. Many nights I remember waking up to the sound of the sirens and running to the shelter across the street. We would gather at the shelter and I'd clutch my doll tightly, huddled close to my mother and waiting for the air raids to stop so that we could return to bed. Each night when I went to sleep, I made sure that I had my robe and shoes by the foot of my bed in case of an air raid. And most of all, I made sure that my doll Erini was there close to me.

When we left Serres with a small suitcase each, we had no room to bring toys and especially my favorite doll. So while in Athens, I begged my mother to get me a doll for Christmas. After my persistent asking, she consented, and even crocheted a beautiful pink dress for my new doll. I named her Erini, which, in Greek, means peace. That doll came with me to the States, and I still have her after seventy-two years. She is in terrible shape, missing a few body parts, thanks to my cousin Costas, who managed to chew off her left arm and right hand. She still has that beautiful baby face, so sweet, that gave me so much comfort during those painful war years.

Air raids continued after we moved to Salonica. The Germans were still there and now the British were the ones bombarding the German camps, while trying to avoid hitting people's homes. We decided that there was no point in going to the shelters anymore. I remember seeing the bombs exploding in the sky and hiding nervously behind a chair, while at the same time being fascinated by their fireworks-like effect. But what I feared most about those years were the Germans themselves: I feared that they would imprison or torture us. I don't remember thinking much about death or dying. I attribute that to my mother, a stoic, who made us feel deeply loved and protected.

Life in Salonica:
The War Years and After (1941–1951)

We moved permanently to Salonica in 1941 because my father had been sent there as a commissioned officer at the onset of the war. We rented a small apartment on the second floor of a two-story house, where I lived until 1951, when I left Greece for the U.S. For a number of years, my father and brother had one of the bedrooms, my grandparents occupied another, and my uncle Vassilis and cousin John shared the third bedroom. My mother and I slept on the dining room table. Somehow this didn't seem strange to me; there was simply no other place we could sleep.

I was very close to my grandmother, Eleni. I was named after her and I identified with her. I wanted to eat whatever she ate and do whatever she did. Living in the same house as my grandparents during those war years was a positive experience for me, and my interactions with them are still vivid. Being around the extended family was also a great source of security.

Grandfather Yannis was ill for most of the time we lived together. He was bedridden, but we three grandchildren—my brother, Cousin John, and I—would visit him in his room whenever he called us with a bribe of some kind of food. He had his way of favoring one of us over the other two by using some special kind of food he had stocked up in his room. He would call out: "Aleco, Eleni, Yanni (whomever he wanted to visit with at that time), I have a piece of loukanico, or some loukoumi for you." Loukanico is a Greek sausage and loukoumi (loucoum) is a Turkish delight.

My grandfather was a handsome man and remained a dandy up to his last breath. As sick as he was—he had cirrhosis of the liver— he would shave regularly, comb his white hair, and brush his mustache. He always had a flower on his lapel. Both of my grandparents died during that time in Salonica. My grandfather died right in the house. I remember seeing him lying in his coffin, which was placed in the middle of the living room, looking peaceful and still handsome. Many friends and relatives came to pay their respects to him. We served food and Metaxa, a Greek cognac. I do not remember anyone crying—it was more like a celebration of his life and who he was. Living a full life to an old age and dying in his own bedroom was, as many visitors said, the wish we all have about our end-of-life.

I am sure that childhood memory has influenced me and the way I feel about death. I don't seem to fear death or worry about death and the aftermath. My fears are more about suffering, being ill, in pain. Or dying before I see my three granddaughters go to college or grow beyond their teenage years. They give me so much pleasure that I hate the thought of parting from them.

My grandmother suffered a stroke and died a few years later. Grandmother was small, standing at just barely five feet. But despite being such a tiny person, she possessed a wealth of knowledge and wisdom. Every member of the extended family talked about her with respect bordering on reverence. She was nicknamed "Venizelos" by her children. Venizelos was a highly regarded Greek politician, smart and charismatic. For me, it was the close relationship I had with her that I so cherished. She would ask me to clean the house with her or sit down and have our breakfast together. She had lost all of her teeth, so she used to mush her bread into her cup of coffee. Sitting next to her, I would imitate her by using a cup of milk with a drop of coffee and mush my own bread in the coffee. We would sit by the kitchen table having our morning coffee, chatting away like two best friends.

After she suffered a stroke, my grandmother was hospitalized. I visited her often, sitting by her bed and telling her stories, which she loved. The night she died, I was sitting next to her, reading to her, but I left the hospital before she took her last breath.

During the war years when we lived in Salonica, electricity and water were scarce. Most of the time we did our homework by kerosene lamplight. Being able to bathe was a treat and unwashed dishes were used for more than one meal. They were marked so that each one of us had our own dish, which we would use for two or three meals before washing. My schooling was highly inconsistent. We would attend classes periodically when space was available, often just for a few hours in the evening. School space was limited because the Germans had taken over a number of public buildings and converted them into office spaces or barracks. Although my school operated with limited resources and frequent interruptions, I still learned a great deal. I was disciplined in my studies and homework. Both of my parents always expected me to do well in school, and I did. While my father was my academic mentor and more involved with my schooling, my mother was more concerned with teaching me all the social graces.

My ancestral background has been important in the way I have been wired. From my mother's side, I have inherited the fighting, my need for freedom, the way I don't accept subordination, or any form of discrimination. My maternal great-great grandparents were fighters in the wars with Turkey during the eighteenth and nineteenth centuries. I feel proud to count among my ancestors such celebrated Greek warriors as the Boukouvalas clan. There have been seventy-five folk songs written about them and a street in Athens is named in honor of one of them, John Boukouvalas. Thinking of this heritage not only makes me feel a great deal of pride, but also a sense of responsibility to be vigilant about the importance of fairness and liberty and the need to fight for one's freedom and independence.

From my father's side, I inherited a love of learning and an interest in intellectual pursuits. All four of my paternal grandmother's brothers had been high achievers: an outstanding mathematician, a professor of economics at Columbia University, an inventor, and a diplomat who served as the Greek ambassador to England during World War II.

The Jews of Salonica

On February 6, 1943, an order was issued for the deportation of the Jews in Salonica. Their stores and they themselves were marked, and they were ghettoized. The first deportation occurred a week later, and by August of that year, 46,000 Salonican Jews had been deported to Auschwitz.

One morning I stood on Evzonon Street near our house witnessing a group of Jews being taken away to concentration camps. They were standing on the street, four in each row, wearing stars on their sleeves and holding small bags with some of their belongings. Their faces were drawn. On each side they were surrounded by German soldiers. Soon word was out that they were going to be burned, and I overheard the whispered speculations that the Germans were going to make soap and lampshades of their remains. It did not make any sense to me, the child that I was. The Jews' houses remained empty, but many of their belongings they had been forced to leave behind were taken by the Greeks. A deprived, hungry child longing for pretty things, I took a beautiful silk dress and a pair of patent leather shoes that lay at the entrance of a house. Looking back, I recognize the sharp disconnect between the shock and sorrow I felt watching their deportation and my yearning for some new clothes. To this day, whenever I see a movie or read anything about the Holocaust, that image of the Jews flashes back to me: the street, their sad and frightened faces, the harshness of the German soldiers.

The Civil War (1946–1949)

The Civil War that followed the German occupation was economically and emotionally devastating for Greece. As soon as the Germans occupied Greece in 1941, a resistance movement was formed, primarily by Communists. They organized up in the mountains with the primary purpose of fighting the Germans. However, the first signs of the Civil War between the leftists and rightists occurred as early as 1942-1944. The rightists, known as the Greek Government Army, were supported by the British and the Americans, while the Democratic Army of Greece (the Communist and socialist resistance fighters) were backed by the Bulgarians, Albanians, and Yugoslavians. The Civil War left Greece even more depleted economically and emotionally and also created in the populace an anticommunist sentiment that led to the Greek Military Junta, which ruled from 1967 to 1974, and the fall of the monarchy.

My personal experience of discomfort during the Civil War was minimal. Most of the actual war erupted in Athens around 1946, while our family lived in Salonica. And the Greeks who suffered the most were the ones who lived in mountainous village areas, where the andartes (resistance soldiers) hid and organized. Villagers said that the Communists were abducting children and putting them in indoctrination camps in neighboring Communist countries. It has been estimated that 30,000 children and teenagers were involved. I remember stories told by newly arrived high school classmates from those villages who had managed to escape. Their stories were frightening—they told how they hid for days at a time in closets, remaining silent in hopes that the andartes would not discover them.

My Parents

My mother Soteria grew up in a well-to-do family. Her father was a successful merchant. As an adolescent and young woman she learned to play the violin and to speak French. I never heard her play the violin, but I did hear her speak French, mostly when she first met my mother-in-law. Communicating with my mother-in-law required some other language besides the limited English my mother had learned back home. So her French came in handy. She never went to college; she got a certificate from an academy for girls, a sort of finishing school.

My mother was attractive and elegant, and she loved beautiful things. Even with limited resources during the war, she managed to keep the home looking beautiful by having fresh flowers in the house, whenever she could afford to buy them. Because of her aristocratic flair, my cousins and other relatives nicknamed her the "princess." She had that air about her—exquisite taste in clothes, decorating, and entertaining. Younger women loved her company and she had numerous young friends, especially after I left home for the U.S. Not surprisingly, a number of men who were friends of the family had crushes on her. Not only was she physically attractive, she was also fun to be with.

My mother was wise and strong. Reflecting back, I am amazed at how she handled the news when I called to tell her that I had met the guy I was going to marry. This guy was Sandy (Alexander), who, at this writing, has been my husband of fifty-eight years.

From the beginning, my mother had opened up her heart to my marrying an American and remaining in the U.S. I first wrote to my parents about Sandy shortly after I had gone out on my first date with him. I reported that I had gone out with this "very tall man," an American classmate, and that I liked him a lot. Not long afterward, I wrote them again, telling them that I was going to marry this "very tall man." I waited anxiously for their response, worried they would disown me. But instead, I got a beautiful letter from my mother about how happy she was that she was going to have a second son. She only wanted to know Sandy's nationality and religion. I wrote back that he was "a little bit English, a little bit Irish, and a little bit Scottish." I also told them that he was Unitarian, and waited again for another letter. How would they feel about a religion that was hardly known in Greece? My mother replied, "I checked with some friends about the Unitarian faith and they said that the 'Unitarians are very good people.'" I could not believe my eyes. I kept reading and rereading the letters. Am I reading them right, that my parents did not get mad at me, disapproving of "my crazy decision" to marry someone I had gone out with only a few times? And also, that it meant that I was going to stay in the States permanently? A few years later, I asked my mother about her beautiful letter that took me so much by surprise. Her response was: "I cried a lot, but I was not going to say or do anything that was going to alienate you or Sandy." That was my mother with her remarkable wisdom.

My father Pericles was born and raised in a small town in Asia Minor and left his hometown to pursue further education at The Polytechnic Institute in Athens. His first language was Turkish and his Greek was limited. He came to Greece alone, a pattern I followed when I left Greece for the U.S. He was working in Serres as a civil engineer when my mother's brothers introduced him to my mother with hopes of having them marry, the typical arranged marriage for those days. I know little about how they finally met each other in person or hardly anything about their courtship. They married in

1926, when my mother was nineteen years of age and my father thirty-two, and settled in Serres.

My father was a mild man, a shy, intellectual type whose hobbies were reading, writing, and listening to classical music. His social life was limited to family outings and occasional get-togethers with one of my uncles. His writing was something he did in private and he told us that he was preparing a technical monograph—work that he never shared with any of us. Neither my brother nor I ever found any part of the monograph after he passed. How did it vanish? Maybe it only existed in his hopes or in a few pieces of scrap paper.

My father also loved to write in the margins of his dictionary about other meanings of words, filling numerous pages in the dictionary with precise small writing. On occasion, he would also include the meaning of the word in German or English—meticulous work that for some reason gave him pleasure. Alex managed to find this dictionary and he brought it back with him to the States.

My father always stayed home when the rest of the family took vacations during the summer months. His excuse was, "I have work to do." In retrospect, I think it had to do with his shyness and the hermit style of life he preferred. He was a soft-spoken man and I never remembered him raising his voice at us—the children or his wife. His family meant everything to him. He rarely indulged in things for himself. His salary and earnings belonged to all of us. During the war years, he would bring home his entire salary in cash and put it in an old red chocolate box, our family bank. All of us had access to it for whatever we needed, and we never abused this privilege. We knew that it was to be used for the family's needs, school supplies, and for a treat here and there. I remember my mother asking, "How are you going to survive in America without the little red box?" While this manner of family finance isn't typical in most families, I believe it instilled a sense of respect and responsibility in my brother and me.

In my father's eyes, I could do no wrong. When I practiced the piano scales, he would praise me for how wonderful they sounded. He would come into my room in the morning and sing to me to wake me up for school. He was my alarm clock, a loving father who woke me up ever so gently. One day I came home from school and told him about an incident with my math teacher. While solving a math problem, I used a different approach than what we'd been taught. I got the right answer, but my teacher wasn't happy about it because I didn't follow his approach to the solution. My father, who excelled in math, being a civil engineer, looked at my solution and said, "Lena, yours is a much more elegant one."

To my father, I was perfect. He never lifted a finger to me. I don't remember ever being punished by him. It was my mother who set the limits and the boundaries for us. He seemed to favor me much more than he did my brother. My father, being such a quiet man, was difficult for Alex to interact with. But, for me, his approval and affection was what I needed and have appreciated over the years. I couldn't have asked for a better father.

My mother expressed more positive, supportive feelings toward my brother, while our own relationship was an intense one. Because both of us were strong-minded and quite stubborn, we had many arguments and often got angry with each other. I am sure she had reason to be upset with me more than once. At the same time, I have fond memories of her waiting for me to come home from school, and sitting beside her to relate everything that had happened that day. She always listened attentively, happy to be a part of my life and experiences.

My father became ill with colon cancer in the mid-1950s. He did not have chemotherapy or radiation; no treatment other than a colostomy. He lived for about six or seven years before he passed in January 1962, during a surgery for his cancer. My brother Alex, who had become a doctor and was living in Vancouver at the time, went to Greece to be present during the surgery. He was the one who called me early the next morning to tell me the sad news. I was still asleep with our second son Paul, who was less than a year old and sleeping in a bassinet next to us. I was devastated but I hardly cried. I had a heavy heart and a pain in my chest. After I had left Greece in 1951, the time I spent with my father was rare and precious. I saw him once when I came home in 1955, again when Sandy and I visited Greece in 1958, and for a third time when our first son John was about six or seven months old, in early spring of 1960. My father was not doing well and I felt that I needed to go and see him. I also knew how eager he was to meet his first grandchild.

One morning I was sitting in the family room holding baby John in my lap. My father looked at us, gave a big smile, and broke into a dance in front of us, singing in Turkish. John started to clap his little hands. My father was so happy to meet Johnny and to have us both there during this hard time with his illness. He couldn't contain himself. He was euphoric. I'm glad I made the trip, as difficult as it was traveling to Europe with an infant. In those days, we did not have the conveniences that we have now in taking care of babies. During the flight, I had to hold John on my lap and I had to bring along baby food (Greece did not carry Dr. Gerber's little food jars). Throwaway diapers did not exist, so I had to carry cloth ones, which my mother washed and ironed lovingly. I wished my father had lived long enough to see me become an academic, a distinguished professor, and a published author. He would have been so proud of me.

After my father passed away, Alex decided to bring my mother back to Vancouver with him. She herself had not been feeling well. She suffered indigestion and stomach pains, but most of the exams suggested stomach ulcers, not a surprising diagnosis given what she was going through with my father's illness. Alex had his colleagues at the University of British Columbia Medical Center do the necessary diagnostic work. Again, the diagnosis was ulcers. The decision was made to operate on her, so I flew to Vancouver to be with them. The operation was successful and things looked promising until Alex did the pathology tests. We got in the elevator, he looked at me, and with a shaky voice said, "Lena, she has stomach cancer." We both were stunned. How could it be? Our father had just died a month earlier from cancer. But fate does not pay attention to such details.

She was always such a strong woman. She took life, with all its good moments and happiness, as well as the pain and suffering, in stride. No complaints. Her motto was to enjoy the gifts you have been given and withstand whatever misfortune and pain you encounter with dignity and patience.

After recuperating from her surgery in Vancouver, our mother moved back to Salonica. She made it a point to visit us once a year, each time spending a month with me and a month with Alex. She loved being with my two young boys. After I left Greece, she had decided to take English lessons so that she could learn enough to communicate with the boys. During her first visit, Paul was about one year old and John about two and a half. She loved to read them the Dr. Seuss books, so when they would come downstairs in their pajamas to kiss us goodnight, she would exclaim, "There come 'Thing One' and 'Thing Two.'"

As her illness continued to progress, Mother started to feel pain all over her body. The cancer had metastasized to her bones. Alex went to Greece in June 1965 with his wife Marcia to bring Mother back to Pittsburgh where they had moved, and where they then both worked as medical doctors. That was my mother's final trip to America. She spent the next six months in and out of the Pittsburgh hospital where my brother worked. She was in excruciating pain, being treated with radiation and painkillers. At the time, we were living in

Washington, D.C., so I was able to visit her often. In the final couple of months, I made the trip from Washington to Pittsburgh every weekend.

As my mother's condition worsened, I spent more time by her bedside. On Christmas Eve 1965, she went into a coma, but occasionally would come out of it. At one point, she opened her eyes and said, "Lena, you need to send some flowers to Peggy [Sandy's mother]." I asked her why and she answered, "Because it's Christmas," before falling back into her coma.

I went home to Washington on Christmas Day morning, surprising Sandy and the children, who were excited to see me. After spending Christmas Day in D.C., Sandy and I flew back to Pittsburgh. I called Alex from the airport to let him know that we had arrived and he broke the news in typical medical style: "Mother just expired."

When we arrived at the hospital, I kissed my mother goodbye. Her cheeks were still warm. Our memorial celebration was just the four of us—Sandy, Marcia, Alex, and I, sharing dinner and playing her favorite music, light operettas.

While mother was sick, I took the kids along to Pittsburgh a couple of times to visit her in the hospital. During our visits, she made sure she was all prettied up and out of bed. She did this for the boys, smiling at them in spite of her excruciating pain. Up until her last days, she asked the nurses to bleach the hair on her upper lip, and they complied with her desire to keep looking pretty. She was a lot like her father, who had died clean-shaven with a well-shaped mustache and beautiful hair parted down the middle.

My Brother and I

When I was growing up, I had enormous admiration for my brother, especially because I felt he was so smart and well read. He was my hero, and I wasn't shy about telling him that. Ironically, as we got older, he admitted that I had become his hero. It was important for me to hear that. We always have respected one another, and while we have remained noncompetitive to this day, as kids we had our moments. He teased me a lot, just like many older brothers do, but he never laid a hand on me. I did feel some elements of sibling rivalry, though. If I got upset or angry, sometimes I would throw things at him. During one family dinner, Alex started to tease me again. Angry, I picked up my soup spoon and threw it across the table, aiming at him. It missed, but I managed to break the window. I must have repressed the consequences I suffered from that behavior. At other times, if I wanted his attention and he had to study, I would start practicing the piano—anything I could do to annoy him.

During one of her visits to America, I told my mother that I always felt she hadn't given me enough praise, and that she had been much more supportive of Alex, especially when it came to our school performance. She explained that her reasoning was that things seemed to come much easier for me, and that Alex had to put forth much greater effort to succeed as much as I had. So she thought that he needed the extra reinforcement. I did not feel that he studied any harder than I did, but he shared my mother's impression of me. He used to say, "Lena, how do you expect to become a scientist? You do not work hard enough." Though I know that my mother felt she was doing the right thing, it often left me feeling unsure of myself and my abilities. I wondered: Do I really deserve the high grades I get?

Alex came to the U.S. in December 1955 to complete his internship. He later completed his medical residency at a hospital in Texas. He had already finished medical school and had served in the Greek Army, and was fluent in English and German. In Greece, part of becoming an educated person was to learn a foreign language. My parents wanted me to do that as well. But frequently I would say to them, "I do not need to learn another language, I play piano."

Like me, Alex arrived from Europe by boat. Sandy and I met him at the dock in New York City. Since he had been traveling around Europe for a while before sailing for the U.S., he had not heard yet that I had fallen in love with Sandy and that we had plans to marry. When I announced to him that the tall, handsome man beside me was my fiancé, he was quite surprised and upset, and walked away without saying a word. Feeling that the decision had been made in haste, when he returned he pulled me aside and asked, "What's your hurry?" I explained that we were in love and I saw no reason to wait. This encounter made me nervous that these two important men in my life wouldn't have the brotherly relationship that I'd been hoping for, but, through the years, a fine and loving relationship developed. Not only do Sandy and Alex love each other, they also have great respect for one another and enjoy each other's company greatly.

Sandy and I married a little less than two months after Alex's arrival. Alex was present at our wedding, the only member of my immediate family. He spent his internship year from 1956-1957 in Washington, D.C. at a hospital not far from where we lived. This allowed Alex and me to rekindle our sibling relationship, and for Sandy and Alex to develop their close friendship.

Alex married Marcia, an attractive pediatrician, during the summer of 1964. The four of us have spent numerous vacations together traveling to Greece and other parts of Europe, Canada, and the U.S. Marcia became the sister I never had. We loved each other's company, enjoyed going shopping together, and talked and laughed. Our taste in clothes, jewelry, and decorating was similar. We both enjoyed Talbot's classical clothes for professional women. She used to love to shop at the Pittsburgh Museum for the arty jewelry pieces she would find for me. The vases, bowls, and casseroles she gave us were in exquisite taste, and to this day, in looking at all these beautiful pieces around the house, I feel her presence, every moment.

In one of our Greek trips, she and I went with our cousin Ioanna to our favorite jewelry store, Lalaounis. Marcia had lost one of the earrings she had bought there and hoped she could replace it. She was taking her time; she was like that, slow and deliberate in everything she did. While she was deliberating, I came across a simple but elegant eighteen-carat gold choker. I tried it on. It looked perfect on my tanned skin and with the deep blue blouse I was wearing. I had to have it. It was expensive, but I could not resist it. Marcia was shocked that I would consider buying such an expensive item, especially doing it on my own without Sandy there. "Okay, Marcia," I said, "I'll call Sandy, let him know, and see what he says." Sandy's response was, "If you like it, get it. Just give a couple of speeches, and that can pay for it." Sandy has always loved to buy jewelry for me. So I did buy it, to the dismay of Marcia. Ioanna, my Greek cousin, was totally amused about the whole thing. I have worn that necklace ever since and love whenever I put it on. A friend of mine calls it my signature piece.

– * –

You will note that I write of Marcia in the past tense; sadly, she died in January 2009, after suffering terribly for five years in a battle with a rare degenerative neurological disease. Watching her body deteriorate was painful. During the last few years of her illness, I was able to go to Pittsburgh at least twice a year to spend time with her. During my last couple of visits to the nursing home where she lived, I found her unable to talk or do anything on her own, her body contorted, crying. All I could do for her was to be there, rub her deteriorating body with lotion, massage her feet, and try to feed her.

Alex has remained in Pittsburgh and now resides at an assisted living facility—an interim or perhaps permanent arrangement. His health and overall emotional state are poor; he feels lonely and isolated, relying for companionship only on occasional interactions with other residents at the facility. We talk on the phone at least once a week, but the distance between L.A. and Pittsburgh makes it difficult for us to see each other in person.

Religion and My Adolescence

It was my brother who first decided to explore religion in greater depth, and who introduced me to a serious practice of my faith. I grew up practicing the Greek Orthodox faith. Religion played a significant role for me during my adolescent years. My parents were not particularly religious; the Greeks have a mentality that resembles the way many Italians practice Catholicism—you go to church on big holidays, but it's not something you necessarily practice on a regular basis.

During the 1940s, a Christian movement emerged in Greece— sort of like born-again Christians, but not quite as fundamentalist. It was much more about living in a truly Christian way and emphasized how to be loving and caring toward others. My brother began practicing their philosophy first, and since I often tried to imitate him, I decided I would join, too. I became a member when I was twelve years old and continued to be involved with the group until I left Greece. As a member, I read the New Testament on a regular basis, attended meetings, practiced confession, and took communion. The key message of the movement was about the importance of "loving thy neighbor" and caring about others. Little attention was paid to the idea of sin or the need for redemption. With little focus on sin, there was also less guilt associated with the practice of my faith. I remember attending an Episcopalian service during my search for a church to affiliate with in the U.S. and feeling amazed by how much emphasis was placed on the notion of viewing ourselves as sinners and the need for salvation. None of my religious experiences in Greece were like this; they focused instead on love and how one can work toward becoming a better person. I remember the first thing I did when I joined the movement was to memorize the epistle from St. Paul to the Corinthians about love. It was my favorite piece in the New Testament.

Another aspect of the movement was service work. We would get products from the UNRRA (United Nations Relief and Rehabilitation Administration) and bring them to be distributed in underprivileged villages. The UNRRA was founded in 1943 to give necessities to areas that had experienced severe loss because of the Axis Occupation. This was the first time I understood the importance of serving others and learning from them. One of the excursions was to a small, remote village north of Salonica. Their homes had been completely destroyed during the civil war. I remember visiting a particular family that was living in a stable. The first thing they said as we arrived was, "What can we serve you?" They were the ones who were suffering, but they wanted to serve us, whether it was just a glass of water or something sweet to eat. What a loving reciprocity of caring for the "other."

Despite all of these positive experiences with the movement, there were also some aspects of the practice that I had a hard time accepting. For example, the idea that we should not pay attention to the way we look: we should dress humbly—no colorful or fashionable clothing, no makeup or jewelry. I remember feeling conflicted because I wanted to look pretty. I wanted to dress up, so I did it anyway. I was reprimanded a couple of times by the superiors in the movement for not being compliant.

When I took my first trip back home in the summer of 1955, now studying in an American graduate school, I went to visit Father

Leonedas, the head of the movement in Salonica. I decided that I would dress and look as I did back in the States. So I wore a cotton polka dot dress with a white color. I had on a pair of dangling earrings and bright red lipstick. While I was trying to make a statement about feeling liberated from the dress code imposed by members of the movement, and also communicate that I did not feel that I had to dress like a nun to feel committed to the principles of my faith, mainly, I wanted to see him and tell him about my life in the States. He was wonderful and nonjudgmental. He listened attentively and was happy to hear about my passion for college and academic learning.

My experiences in the Christian movement in Greece helped me to understand and practice my faith at a deeper level. That has played a crucial role in my development and the person that I have become. For that, I'm immensely grateful.

High School (1942–1949)

I attended an all-girl high school, which in Greece is referred to as "gymnasium," for eight years, following four years of elementary school. Though it was a public high school, we had to wear uniforms, black ones with white collars. Not having enough money for uniforms, my mother took the black lining out of one of her coats and made me one. A few years later, after the occupation had ended, she somehow got hold of some new silk material and made me this gorgeous black silk uniform; perhaps she got the silk from UNRRA. My first "new" coat was made from materials that had also been sent over from the U.S. My first new pair of shoes, white oxfords, was sent from the U.S. The first time I tasted peanut butter was from a jar that had been sent from the U.S. In my teenage years, these simple pleasures were my first strong connection to the United

States. I didn't know much about America, but I imagine that what must have attracted me to this country early on might have been the fact that we were receiving all these things that we so desired but could not have. I developed the notion that this new and exciting country had lots of wealth, but that it was also a country that cared greatly about others.

I was an excellent student in high school, the quintessential teacher's pet. All of my teachers liked me, and I admired most of them. I was especially fond of my writing and literature teacher—a superb teacher and a beautiful woman with a kind face. Her hair was pulled back and she wore light-colored rimmed glasses. She was my hero. I graduated from high school with the perfect grade of 20 (equivalent to 100% in the U.S.) in every course. Since I was a top student, I was given the special honor of carrying the Greek flag during parades and other events and celebrations. This experience must have played a role in making me feel highly patriotic, but my husband Sandy has made an interesting observation about Greek patriotism: Greeks have a way of talking about how wonderful Greece is, yet Greek people don't make comparisons about being better than any other country or other people. It's just a confident feeling that we're "good."

After the German occupation ended in 1944, my high school education resumed with some reasonable normalcy. I received an excellent education in spite of the hard times during the war years, when we lacked classroom space and suffered from uncertainty as to when classes could meet. Often, we had to meet in the evenings. Learning ancient Greek and being able to read Plato, Aristophanes, Euripides, and others in the original text was a significant experience. I may not have realized it then, but looking back, I believe that these great philosophers had a large impact on me. Socrates' "the unexamined life is not worth living" (which in the Greek text reads *ou to zin, alla to eu zin*) has remained with me throughout my life as the motto that guides me. It's not just living, but living meaningfully, that matters.

While we were reading Homer's Odyssey in its original language in my literature class, the teacher stopped at the section where Helen of Troy makes an appearance. All the old men were sitting at the Coliseum, and one of them proclaims: "For such a woman the war is worth it." Our teacher pointed out that Homer was able to communicate Helen's beauty without describing any specific attributes: hair color, eyes, figure. And he continued, "…with the statement from one of the elders, the reader gets the essence of her beauty. One can imagine how she looks without any specific description of her looks… For such a woman the war is worth it."

Growing up in Greece, I had no exposure to popular media: movies, TV, or fashion magazines. Thus I had no particular sense of what constitutes female beauty as it appears in popular culture. I grew up believing that one develops her own sense of beauty and of what constitutes attractiveness. I never worried about how I looked. I felt attractive and had no concerns about body image, weight issues, or overall appearance. "Beauty is in the eye of the beholder." Homer's Helen of Troy revisited.

I was particularly strong in math and science. My writing was always clear but short and precise. I didn't have much literary imagination and did not enjoy novels, which might explain how I came to be a researcher. Early on, I wanted to become an architect, but when I was studying to enter the university, I decided I would rather study physics. My parents discouraged me concerning both options, feeling that architecture and physics were not appropriate for women. My father said, "Lena, you're not going to have an easy time in those careers. They're male occupations, and I don't think it's the best thing for you." A civil engineer himself, he advised that if I were to become an architect, I'd be the only woman, and that would not be a comfortable career experience for me. Instead, both of my parents felt that becoming a teacher was the appropriate career for a woman in case she needed to work someday and earn a living.

And so, after the gymnasium, I ended up going to the teacher's college for a two-year program. I didn't particularly enjoy it, except for one course in psychology. Psychology as a subject of interest must have been in my DNA. When I was around fourteen, I found a copy of the Stanford-Binet Intelligence Scales that had been translated into Greek on my uncle's bookshelf. I took it down and went around the neighborhood asking all the kids the test questions. I was a psychologist in the making.

In high school, I also became interested in career development and how people choose their life's work. I am not sure where that came from, although the conversations I had with my parents about my career choices, and their comments about the appropriateness of occupations for women, played a role. I remember reading books about career choice when I was fifteen or sixteen years old. Perhaps in a subliminal way, I was aware of gender discrimination when it came to what occupations women should choose and enter, and was tuned into these issues early on in life. My undergraduate honors thesis at Adelphi University was about how women choose their majors in college and what role the parents play in that choice. It was fresh in my mind, having given up on my dream to become an architect or physicist and instead becoming a schoolteacher.

I also observed early on the gender-related choices men and women were making. My mother took care of the home responsibilities and my father was the breadwinner. My father wasn't a particularly macho man; he was actually soft. It was my uncle who lived with us who spanked me once, and, I might add, pretty hard. One night I came home late after an excursion with my cousin, his son, to observe the religious celebrations on Good Friday. In Greece, you have a mock funeral on Good Friday; the clergy and parishioners go around the neighborhood simulating Christ's funeral. My cousin John and I had decided to visit every church we could to see how it was done. We didn't get home until one o'clock in the morning, and my uncle was furious. As far as he was concerned, girls were not supposed to be out late at night, alone or not. He didn't hit his son, but he hit me. He took a look at me and said with a harsh voice, "Lena, what were you doing, late at night, wandering around the streets?" The fact that I was safely with his son and that we were participating in a religious experience did not matter. All that mattered to him was that a young girl should not be out late at night. Those differential treatments of men and women had an impact on me that I'm sure influenced my feminist views and life's work.

Besides my mother's older sister, who became a schoolteacher, none of the women from my mother's generation attended college. By contrast, all of my mother's brothers were college-educated. That pattern was similar with my father's family. My grandmother didn't go to college, but all of her brothers were highly educated and successful. However, Greek women of my generation were supported academically and in pursuing careers. Among my cousins, all of the women are university graduates. One of them became dean of a two-year college and her two sisters are both pharmacists. My parents supported my coming to this country for higher education, and they remained supportive of my working even when I had young children. After my second pregnancy, I stopped working for a while because we moved and I thought it was unwise to get another job when I knew I was going to have another baby. My mother wrote to me all the way from Greece asking, "Why did you get all of these degrees? Just so you could change diapers?" On the other hand, my mother-in-law was ambivalent about my working once I had kids.

My Music Conservatory Years

Music has always been central in my life. When we returned from Athens to Salonica, I kept insisting that I wanted to start piano lessons again, but my parents said that they couldn't afford lessons or a piano for me to use for practice at home. In order to get what I wanted, I threatened them that if I couldn't take piano lessons I would stop eating. Finally, they succumbed. Since we did not have a piano at home and couldn't afford to buy one, we rented time from a neighbor who owned one for me to practice. I must have been around eleven or twelve years old when I started piano lessons for the second time, and I studied until I left Greece at age nineteen. I attended the Greek Conservatory of Music (while in high school), and I had become quite advanced before I moved to this country. Had I gone on for two or three more years, I would have had my certificate in piano. In addition to piano lessons, my music training included solfeggio, harmony, theory, and the history of music. It was a total immersion into music, and I loved everything about my years at the Conservatory.

Often, I would arrive early for my piano lesson so that I could hear the advanced students perform their pieces for Miss Thoula, our piano teacher. I particularly remember one of the male students who was exceptionally talented—a tall, gangly boy of about thirteen. He came from a gypsy family and his father would come to the Conservatory to hear him perform. On my way to high school, I walked through his neighborhood, a small enclave of gypsy families living in shacks that weren't well maintained. But then I would overhear the fabulous piano music that poured out of his family's little bungalow.

The years I spent at the Greek Conservatory hold many memories for me, including that of my first romantic love. On my way to the Conservatory, I used to walk the same path, crossing a few busy streets and then an open field. I would arrive, a starry-eyed twelve-year-old, hoping to encounter Mimis, a tall, dark, handsome young man of about sixteen with large dark eyes. This budding violinist was my first crush, and I pined for him the whole time I attended the conservatory. I continued to think of him for a few years after I left Greece. I think he had a crush on me, too, but neither of us ever acknowledged it.

My fantasies about Mimis were only part of my diary and my daydreams. He was my Paganini. I'll never forget the day of my piano recital, when I was about seventeen. By then, he had moved on to the University where he was studying to become a doctor alongside my brother Alex. We were outside in the open space surrounding the conservatory building. He was sitting down, I was standing. We looked at each other. I was nervous about my impending public performance. Without a word, he reached out for my hands, and held them to warm them up. I got nervous and blushed, but I let him hold them. It felt so good; it was an innocent sexual feeling, my first physical contact with my first adolescent love. I wrote to him a couple of times after I came to the U.S., describing my life and experiences here, but never expressing my romantic feelings toward him. He wrote me back. When I went back to Greece in 1955, my friend Afroula arranged for me to see him, though he was sick in bed with pneumonia. That was my last encounter with him. During another visit to Greece, this time with Sandy, I asked Afroula about Mimis. She said that he had been in an automobile accident that left him paralyzed. "You would not want to see him," she said. I will always remember him and what it feels like to have butterflies in your stomach as you experience your first youthful love.

My diary had a short life, only five years or so. One day I learned that my mother had gotten into it. She let it out by teasing me about "my Paganini." I was angry and upset; I took it out of my drawer and, in her presence, threw it into the burning fireplace. I've never kept a diary since that time.

As poor as I was when I moved to the United States, I continued to study piano. I had superb music teachers during my undergraduate years at Adelphi University and as a graduate student at Ohio University, but I knew that playing piano was never going to be my life's work. I was serious about it, but not to the point of wanting to become a concert pianist. When I was at Ohio University, the conductor of the San Francisco Symphony, a Greek-American, came to give a master class in piano and invited me to join. After I performed, he said, "Lena, continue to study and enjoy playing piano, but I don't think that you can become a concert pianist." I told him that that was okay with me, that being a concert pianist wasn't my aspiration anyway. He gave me some sheet music of his own compositions as a gift, which I still have with my piano music collection.

A significant part of my life, music was also what brought Sandy and me together. Music has remained central in our lives and our family. Both of our sons dreamed of and tried to make their livelihood as musicians; today they compose, perform, and produce their own CDs, as an avocation. Even though I stopped taking lessons after my second son was born, I continued to practice and play. Music is everywhere around me. We have a piano in our city home and beach home. We celebrate special occasions, birthdays and anniversaries, with musicales at home. And Sandy plays piano often. The trajectory of my life, from a child in Greece to my eighties in America, has been embellished, enhanced, and enriched by my love of music: to play, to hear, to enjoy.

CHAPTER 2

Coming to America

My parents promised that after I completed my training at the Pedagogical Academy (Teachers' College), I could leave the country to further my education by going to a foreign university, perhaps in Switzerland or France. From the beginning, I knew that I wanted to go to America.

During a trip to Athens to visit relatives, I met Dinos, a friend of my aunt's, a dentist who was sixteen years older than me. A year after I met him, he migrated to the U.S. for further training to become an orthodontist. He was fond of me, so I decided to correspond with him about the possibility of my coming to the U.S. for further studies. Dinos was more than "fond"; he was romantically interested and therefore eager to do everything he could to bring me to the States. He found out about the Anglo-American-Hellenic Bureau of Education, an enterprise that offered scholarships to Greek students for studies at American universities. The Bureau had been established primarily by a group of Columbia University humanities professors who believed that if they were to bring some talented young Greek students to this country, educate them, and then send them back to Greece, they could help rejuvenate the "Golden Age of Pericles." Of the young Greek scholars who came through the Bureau, as far as I know not one returned to Greece.

Dinos sent me all the necessary papers for a scholarship through the Bureau. Mr. Lucas, the director of the Bureau, said that in terms of my academic credentials there would be no problem for me to get accepted. However, I would be responsible for figuring out everything else I would need to do in order to emigrate to the U.S. First of all, I had to be able to speak English well enough to pass a test. I also had to have someone in the U.S. who could put down a $1,000 deposit on my behalf as a type of insurance. That was a lot of money in 1951.

These were two major obstacles. I didn't speak any English, and who could possibly provide me with $1,000? The first thing was to try to find someone who could contribute the money. My grandmother had three brothers in New York City, the Aghnides brothers, all highly educated and accomplished professionally. I had never met any of them and they didn't know anything about me other than that I was their nephew's daughter. That did not stop me. I took it upon myself to write a letter to each one of them telling them that I had been accepted into a program to come to the U.S. as a college exchange student on a scholarship. I described myself along with how badly I hoped to do this, explaining the need for a $1,000 gift, a deposit in my name. I remember my mother saying to me, "Yeah, good luck. Someone who doesn't know you is just going to give you that much money?" Not one, but two of my great uncles went to Mr. Lucas offering to pay the full amount on my behalf.

The first Aghnides great uncle to visit Mr. Lucas with the $1,000 was Elie, who had made a fortune by inventing the faucet aerator.

After I met him, I asked how he'd come up with the idea. "Well, Lena," he said, "I was on a trip to Niagara Falls, and I watched with great fascination as the water hit the rocks with such great force, creating a lot of froth. So, I thought, what if I were to produce a gadget that attaches to faucets and, as the water comes out, creates a lot of bubbles, thus making it softer and more pleasurable to the touch?" And, voilá—an invention that has lasted for decades. Elie was debonair, handsome, cosmopolitan. He lived in New York and Paris, with fabulous apartments in both cities. His New York residence was a corner apartment in the Hotel Pierre, and in Paris, he had a large penthouse on Avenue George V. In the winter, he went to Zermatt to ski, and spent most other holidays in the Caribbean Islands, his favorite being Antigua. He was a ladies' man, always flirting and making a woman feel special, no matter her age.

Thanassis Aghnides, Elie's older brother, also went to Mr. Lucas' office with an offer to sponsor me, but was told that Elie had already taken care of it. Thanassis was a diplomat at the League of Nations in Geneva and later served as the secretary of the International Disarmament Conference. During World War II, he was appointed Greek ambassador in London at the Court of St. James. He completed his diplomatic career by serving as Secretary of Budgetary Concerns at the United Nations.

The eldest of the three brothers was Nicholas, who also lived in New York. He was a professor of economics at Columbia University and an expert in the stock market. He declined the invitation to sponsor me because, he said, he did not have the money due to other family obligations. He was the only married one at the time, but with no children. (They had three cats instead.) Nicholas nonetheless also welcomed me warmly, extending himself more than once by having me to dinner at their apartment and taking me to the New York Stock Exchange. I was fascinated to witness the energy of all the people, mostly men, on the floor as the marquee kept changing, listing various stock values, but completely lost and confused as to what it all meant. Today, I am still confused about it all.

It was not long before a letter arrived from Mr. Lucas, reporting that the money had come through. I ran upstairs out of breath to read it to my mother. She started to cry.

"I never expected that it was a real possibility," she said, which is why she had agreed to allow me to apply in the first place. I wasn't sure of it either, but I figured that I had nothing to lose. It was certainly bold of me to write to people I had never met, asking them for that much money. But it worked.

The next obstacle was the English test. I found an English teacher named Lilly, who became a good friend. She was a Greek-American, and she and her family later moved back to the States. Since they lived in Brooklyn, I got to see her while I was attending Adelphi University on Long Island. Lilly and Stellios, her husband, were family to me during my first two years in the States. They fed me and drove me around, exploring different parts of New York City and its surroundings.

After a few years in the States, Lilly and her family returned to Greece, where they remained. I visited them in the early eighties, when Sandy and I spent a three-month sabbatical in a small village outside of Athens. Lilly was in the last days of her life, lying in bed, her body being eaten away by metastasized cancer. Yet she was serene, lying there with a sweet smile on her face. Next to her bed was a small Greek icon of a saint. She wanted to hear all about me, my family, my work, my life, as her husband watched quietly over both of us. Her serenity about her imminent death touched me deeply and has remained vivid: a lesson in how to face death with dignity and equanimity.

– * –

It was already summer and college in the States was going to start in September, so I took only one month of English lessons with Lilly before I had to be tested and leave. When it came time to take the test, I went ahead with it, even though I didn't feel ready. Lilly took me to the American college (Anatolia College) in Salonica near where I grew up. It was a school where Greek students could complete high school while taking an immersion program in English. Soon after we arrived, I realized that my poor English would make it hard for me to pass the test. The school's president, who was an American, felt the same way and said to me, "What are we going to do? You're supposed to be fluent in English before I can certify that you can attend college in the States." My teacher jumped in, telling him how smart I was and that she was sure that I would learn English quickly. To my surprise, he agreed to pass me. Another fluke, another obstacle overcome! It felt like it was meant to be. So there I was, not speaking any English, with a certificate saying that I had passed the test.

Next, I needed to get a passport, a visa, tickets, all the logistics. My parents said that they weren't going to help me with any of this. I had to take care of it by myself, they said, because doing that would assure them that I was able to make it on my own, so far away from home in a foreign country. This challenge was not easy for a girl who had been overprotected all her life. I had never left home, not even for summer camp. Organizing all that had to be done required a lot of work, persistence, and some ingenuity, especially given the Greek bureaucracy, which takes forever to handle paperwork and requires that you visit at least ten offices. But I was determined. I am tenacious, and when I set my mind to do something, nothing stops me.

While my parents supported my efforts to arrange to study abroad, believing strongly as they did in the value of education, my brother was skeptical. He thought I should wait to learn English first. He already spoke English and knew that it was not going to be easy for me to go to a new country and start college without speaking the language.

I did manage to do all of the necessary paperwork; the ticket was purchased and everything was arranged. The day came that I had to leave for America, a major event for an overprotected but not shy nineteen-year-old. By now, my parents were supportive. My mother, who had exquisite taste in clothes, got me a winter coat and a couple of nice dresses. She believed in having only a few things, but made sure that they were well-made with the best possible materials. Her practice was to have one new good dress for the winter and one for the summer, and that was all, but they had to be of high quality.

I came to the U.S. in the summer of 1951 on an Italian ship named LaGuardia. We departed from Piraeus, the port of Athens. My whole family came to the dock to see me off. My mother was crying and I was crying, but I was also excited to be embarking on this adventure, not realizing what it would mean and the hardships I would have to face. I treated it like it was going to be a trip to Athens or another city in Greece. I was going to have a wonderful adventure and I would be able to do new things and have all sorts of exciting experiences. I must say, it was my naïveté that got me through, because anyone with a little more sense would not have done it. They would have waited at least until they had learned to speak English before they made such a major move. That's why, in retrospect, it is beyond me that my parents accepted my decision and trusted me enough to let me go all alone to a new country without enough financial resources and without speaking the language. I often ask myself what it was that drove me to this. Was it the thought of pursuing further education or the adventure of it all? I always loved school and learning, and I think that was a major motivation for me, as well as a big part of my parents' decision to let me go, as well. They would have done anything to help me get more education, to achieve more, and to follow my dreams.

But my yearning for adventure also played a major role, and that adventure began onboard. Other students were emigrating as well, some of them on scholarships from the same Bureau. This was the first time that I felt free to stay up all hours of the night, dance, flirt, and enjoy that freedom. It was an exhilarating experience to be on a ship crossing the Atlantic, feeling so independent. All of the young students stayed in the cheapest cabins, but somehow we managed to find a way to go to the first class for our entertainment. I don't know how we did it, but we would meet there, enjoying the beauty of the surroundings and each other. I felt so grown up. I had a short affair of the heart with a handsome guy, a music lover, who shared with me his experiences of a European trip to Salzburg for the summer music festivals. I listened, starry-eyed. He gave me a picture he had taken there of Mozart's statue. I felt touched that he parted with the only picture of Mozart he had, a memento of his trip to Salzburg. My memory of that short, pleasant interlude, that flirtatious encounter, has remained with me over the years. And Mozart's picture is still in a box of miscellaneous photographs.

The Adventure Begins

I arrived in New York on a gloomy, rainy day. The ship docked at the port and the first thing I saw was the Statue of Liberty, a majestic view. Reality hit me. What was I doing in a new country, all alone, and not speaking English?

I started to cry, feeling apprehensive and full of fear of what was next. But my fears were somewhat eased when we disembarked and were met by a group of Greek students, all members of the Lucas enterprise. They greeted us warmly and enthusiastically suggested that we needed to see the city that evening. Suitcases and all, they took us to Times Square.

What an experience that was! The lights, the noise, the colorful marquees were beautiful and overwhelming. We went to a Greek restaurant, and that felt good, a touch of the homeland. Next they took us to the Radio City Music Hall. I sat there for two hours watching a movie in English. Of course, I did not understand a word, and my anxiety about what was I going to do not speaking English hit me hard, again. How was I going to navigate this new life, new country, a college where I did not know anyone, and take classes without knowing the language?

Among the group of students who welcomed us that first evening was Artemis, a young woman about my age who became one of my closest friends, and who remains so to this day. Right away, she invited me to stay with her in her apartment in the city, near Columbia University. I stayed with her for two weeks, until classes began. The first two things she said to me were: "You need to shave under your arms like the rest of the girls do here"; and "You can't hold my arm when we walk together. In this country, people will think that we are lesbians." She walked with me to the corner drugstore and bought me a shaver: a fast beginning to my acculturation in America. Artemis was a pre-med student at Barnard College. She extended an invitation to me to stay in the Barnard dorm with her any time I came down to the city. And that I did. I spent many weekends in her room, visiting with her and the rest of the Lucas students. I had my Greek community in the city. Besides Artemis and two other Greek women, there were seven to ten young men, all of them attending nearby colleges and universities. All of us had scholarships from the Anglo-American-Hellenic Bureau of Education.

I attended college at Adelphi University, in Garden City, Long Island, which is about half an hour by train from New York City. I was classified as a junior. I got a number of credits transferred from the Greek teacher's college and others from my studies in ancient Greek literature while in the gymnasium.

Whenever I felt lonely, it was easy for me to get the train and meet my group of Greek friends. That gave me a sense of comfort during those first years in this country. Most of us in the group have tried to remain connected over the years. I've been most connected with Artemis because we lived in Washington D.C. at the same time, in the mid-1960s. My sons got to know her daughters, and we all have fond memories of making the traditional Greek sweets, coura-biedes and melomacarona, during the Christmas holidays. I have re-mained in touch with Artemis' oldest daughter Daphne, who has become a producer of documentaries, a feminist, and politically conscious.

After two weeks spent living in Artemis' apartment in the city, I moved into the Adelphi dorms in early September. My roommate, a freshman, was a Jewish girl from Brooklyn. The girls in the dorm floor came to greet me, friendly and talkative, but I could not understand a word. One of them, trying to make conversation, told me that her roommate was Natalie Rose, and asked me who my roommate was. When I heard the word rose, I said to myself, "rose is a flower," so I responded, "mine is carnation." I thought that she was asking about my favorite flower.

What fascinated me about American college girls was the amount of clothes they brought with them. My roommate kept unloading more and more skirts, blouses, and sweaters. Her closet was packed full. I looked at mine. Not much. Just two dresses, one skirt, and a few sweaters.

I had a terrible feeling of not belonging. I was a "foreign student." Everything felt foreign, indeed. Fortunately, I found a group of Greek students on campus who became my "Greek connection," eager to help me with anything I needed. They offered to meet me at registration for classes and walk me through it. I went and waited for one of my new Greek friends to help me, but nobody showed up. So I stumbled through it. I don't know how I managed to do it. I felt disappointed, abandoned, even rejected. It did not make sense to me that they did not keep their promise. Would I be able to trust them again? The next day, when I asked them what happened, they said that they thought that it would be a good idea to let me do it by myself and learn the essential survival skills for college from the start. It was a bit too early for such a lesson, but my hurt feelings did not last long. I soon felt good again to have Greek friends there.

I also made friends with some of the other foreign students who lived in my dorm—a Korean, a German, and a French woman. We were all struggling with adjustment issues, and that connected us into this friendship circle. I lost track of them over the years until recently, when I received a call from Marie-Lise, the French girl. She brought me up-to-date about the rest of the group and their whereabouts. During our conversation, she kept repeating: "Oh Lena, I remember you sitting at the piano in the dorm living-room playing Debussy, so beautiful." We exchanged pictures of each other over email and promised to keep in touch. Her mentioning my playing piano and Debussy brought back many memories, along with sorrow that I had to stop playing the piano after an accident that happened when I was seventy-eight. We were celebrating Christmas dinner at my nephew's home, a joyous occasion for the whole family and friends. I was standing at the top of the stairs when I lost my balance and somersaulted down the staircase, dislocating my shoulder, breaking my humerus, and injuring my brachial plexus. The accident left me with severe neuropathy in my left hand.

Classes at Adelphi began in late September, and, until December, it was hell for me. I was miserable. I got migraine headaches for the first time in my life. One day I tried to get out of bed to get ready for class and felt an excruciating headache. I couldn't even walk to the bathroom. Tears streamed down my face. Of course, I couldn't go to class. I went straight back to bed and waited for it to pass. I was a mess that term: I got styes in my eyes and boils all over my face. My anxiety and discomfort were causing my body to react; I was somatizing all of my emotional pain. Nonetheless, I went to my classes faithfully and sat through the lectures and class discussions, not understanding a word. To cope, I decided to get every textbook on the subject matter of each class, and read my assignment in each one of the three or four textbooks I checked out of the library. I used my Greek-English dictionary to try to translate every word in the assignment. I still have that dictionary, all beaten up from the excessive use I made of it. It remains a memento of those early years of college life.

Before long, I realized that this approach to doing homework was not efficient. I next decided to read the same passage over and over again and see what I could absorb—an interesting way of learning a new language—almost by feeling the meaning of what was there on the printed page. I do that now with French. I try to understand what is said by "feeling it," picking up a few words here and there and using the context to figure out what someone is trying to communicate. This way of doing my homework and beginning to learn the language appeared to work. I was able to manage it, but with difficulty.

Besides having physical problems and hardly understanding what others were saying, I didn't comprehend any of the rules and regulations about residential life. In those days, universities practiced "in loco parentis." We were grounded if we came back to the dorm after hours—and I was guilty of that more than once. I would visit Uncle Pro, a cousin of my father's, who lived near the college. I would get back to the dorm after hours and the housemother would ground me: "Next weekend, you cannot go anywhere, Lena." For the whole semester I felt I was in a rough sea, full of huge waves, struggling to come out of it.

I took three courses during that miserable first semester: a required biology course, an English course for foreign students, and a course in music. I took the music course in the hope that I could understand a little something of what was presented in class. My biology course was my biggest problem. Because I barely understood the lectures, I got an F on the midterm exam. The housemother called me into her office after the results came out and said, "You got an F, what happened?" I didn't know what an F was—that's how out of it I was.

Thank God for Uncle Pro and his family, who became my surrogate family during those two years at Adelphi. Pro was a second cousin of my father's, but he and my father were good friends in Athens while my father was attending the Polytechnic Institute. They even roomed together for awhile. Pro had immigrated to the United States, married an Italian woman named Florence, and adopted a son, Peter. He was a commodities trader, doing pretty well financially. They lived in a town near the college, but also had a small house in the Hamptons. I spent many holidays and summer days with them. They and the Greek students on campus were my anchors.

During the first semester, all I could do was study every hour that I was not in class. I would sit on the end of my bed, next to my desk, and spend hours studying. By the end of the year, the bed was concave at that end, because I hardly moved out of that spot. I did a little socializing with the Greek students, but hardly with any other students, since I could not speak English. But by Christmas, I had started to understand and speak some English. I finished the first semester successfully, passing all of my courses, including biology. Music was my fun course, one that I did not need to worry about. Ironically, the English course for foreign students was not helpful in teaching me the language or in giving me what I needed to know to manage my courses. It was not until the second semester that I finally started to get a sense of what was happening around me and in my courses.

My brother, who all along felt that I did not do much studying while back home, was astonished to learn about all the hours of hard work I put into my studies those early college years. I was determined to succeed and I did. I graduated from Adelphi with high honors (magna cum laude), and years later was inducted in their "Alumni Academy of Distinction."

During those two years at Adelphi, I also had financial hardships to contend with. Yes, I had a scholarship, but I needed to earn money for my room, board, and miscellaneous expenses. Coming out of the war years, Greece would not allow any money to leave the country, so my parents could not help me financially. I had to find my own ways of making some money. I worked in the school cafeteria, and that provided me with board. I did a lot of babysitting during the academic year, and I worked full-time during the summers. Both summers, after my junior and senior years, I managed to hold two jobs at a time. The first summer I lived with a family and took care of their three-year-old for part of the day and evenings, while I also had a job from six o'clock in the morning until three o'clock in the afternoon at a hospital for children with cerebral palsy. I was hired as a nurse's aide, and part of the job was to change the children's diapers. Some of the "children" were teenagers. Every time I had to change a diaper I would end up vomiting. The nurses and administration decided that this job was not going to work for me. But instead of firing me, they reassigned me to a job as a music specialist, entertaining the children with music and song. My musical experience and training came in handy.

The second summer I got a job in Asbury Park, N.J. I lived again with a family where I worked as a babysitter for five children during the day and as a bus girl during the evening at the family's Greek restaurant. The owner of the restaurant was a heavy, unpleasant Greek man who treated his employees and his (non-Greek) wife harshly. With me, he had a different issue. He thought I was uppity and acted too much like a princess. I could not figure out his attitude, given the fact that I worked as a bus girl at his restaurant. I think he resented the fact that I was a college graduate. He would often throw that in my face. When my mother heard about the work I was doing, she got upset and wrote, "Do not tell me what you do. It is too demeaning for you, that restaurant job."

I worked hard both summers, and did manage to earn enough money to cover many of my living expenses while in college. I also had my angels among the faculty and administration. Ruth Harley, the Dean of Students, always looked out for me in terms of getting me scholarships and additional financial aid whenever available and for which I could qualify. Dr. Dorothy Disher, a faculty member who taught child development, took me under her wing. First, she hired me as a research assistant. She could have hired any graduate student in the program, but I believe she did this as a way of helping me financially. One day she called me in her office and presented me with a five hundred dollar check. It was a gift. When I questioned it, she said, "Lena, this money is sitting in the bank. It is a much better use of it for you to have it." I was grateful, deeply touched by her generosity.

After I left Adelphi, I remained in contact with Dr. Disher. She sent us a beautiful platter as a wedding gift. She never married. Perhaps she saw me as the daughter she might have hoped for.

– * –

Other angels looked after me, as well. Ten days after I arrived at Adelphi, I took the train and ventured into the city hoping to find Artemis or any of the friends from my Greek Lucas group. I had not made any arrangements ahead of time about where and when to meet, so I went to Lucas' office. No one was there. I sat at the steps of the building hoping that someone might show up, but no such luck. Back I went to the train station to head back to college. But now I was on the train not knowing where to get off for the college. I turned to the gentleman sitting next to me and with half English, half hand motions, I communicated that I needed to return to Adelphi. At the right station, he motioned to me that we needed to get off. He then hailed a taxi, paid the driver, and asked him to take me to the dorm at Adelphi. I am sure he was worried about this naïve young girl traveling in the night not knowing where she was going. That experience was a gift: it taught me about people's kindness, generosity, and protectiveness—even in a big city like New York.

My Uncle Elie

The first date I made with Uncle Elie was shortly after I arrived from Greece. We were both excited to meet each other. He was filled with anticipation over meeting his nineteen-year-old niece from Greece. He must have had a fantasy of meeting a young, glamorous woman, but instead, he met this naïve, chubby, kid-like young woman who was more like a fourteen-year-old by American standards of sophistication. He was standing outside his apartment waiting for me. He looked at me, his smile faded, and he said, "Before we go into the apartment, let's go to the drugstore at the corner. I want to weigh you. You're very heavy." Some way to meet this important uncle for the first time! We went to the drugstore where he weighed me and announced that I was "overweight."

Not long after our first meeting, Elie called a woman friend and told her, "Take Lena shopping and let her buy anything she needs. Just do whatever she wants." And indeed, she took me to some big stores in New York City, and I got my clothes for college—skirts and sweaters—everything the girls used to wear in the fifties. That was a sweet thing of him to do, after he insulted me about my weight.

Elie was a puzzle. He was hard on me about my weight, yet proud of my academic pursuits. While he would never praise me to my face, he would tell his friends about his wonderful niece, the high achiever. And he was generous. Whenever I met him for dinner in the city, he would always say, "Would you like a little money for the subway?" And he would usually give me fifty dollars, so that I would have some extra money.

One day he called me up and said, "I have a friend of mine visiting me from Belgium, and I would love you to join us for dinner." I said, "I would love to join you!" For a starving college student, going to a nice New York restaurant was special. Then he asked if I spoke French, and when I said that I was learning, he replied, "Then we'll wait until you've learned." He disinvited me just like that. That is who he was. He would say and do things that hurt, while at the same time be generous and caring. Later, after I got married, whenever Sandy and I visited him in Paris, he would go out of his way to do everything he could to show us the best of times.

For my wedding, I asked him to give me away, since my parents were not going to be there. He felt honored, and immediately said yes. He offered to get me anything I needed for the wedding—perhaps money for my wedding gown? I said that I would welcome any help. He said, "Would two hundred dollars do?" I bought a wedding dress for forty-five dollars. (Those were the fifties, and one could get a beautiful dress for that small amount of money.) With the rest, we put a down payment on a piano, the first piano Sandy and I bought together. Elie also asked me what I wanted for a wedding gift. Naively, I answered that we needed some drinking glasses, meaning just some everyday glasses. He went to one of the best stores and sent us two large boxes full of high quality, German-design crystal, twelve of each kind, forty-eight pieces in all. I still have some of them left, fifty-eight years later. They were so thin that most of them broke. You just look at them and they will shatter.

Uncle Elie wanted me to be different: slim, attractive, and much more sophisticated than I was. For my part, I liked his creative mind, his style, and his sophistication. He patronized the best restaurants in Paris and New York City. He dressed exquisitely. He visited me only once in Los Angeles. During the visit, after breakfast, he would put on his cashmere coat and walk back and forth on our pool deck. Gwyn, a daughter of friends who was visiting us at the same time, took one look at him, and with a laugh said, "Where is his butler?" That says it all.

Elie married only once, when he was in his late fifties, to a woman of twenty-eight. He made sure that if I were asked about his age I should say that he was forty-two. He called me up one evening and said, "Lena, I want you to meet me for dinner. I want to introduce you to someone." I took the train from college and met them in his apartment. She was a beautiful graduate student at Columbia University, tall, with flame-red hair, wearing a white mink stole around her neck and five-inch heels. She smoked cigarettes using a cigarette holder. I looked at her with awe. When we were ready to go to dinner, she turned to me and said, "Wherever Lena wants to go to dinner, we should go there," as though I knew New York and the fancy restaurants well enough to make the decision.

They went for their honeymoon to the French Riviera. A week or so later, I got a note from her thanking me for the wedding gift I had sent them, a set of records of Strauss' Fledermaus. When she wrote, "I'm sure this will be a great addition to Elie's collection," I said to myself, "This doesn't sound good." I called him up and he told me that they had split—she had left him during the honeymoon. His story was that she didn't want to have children, while he wanted to.

When Elie passed away at age ninety-three, he left everything in both of his apartments, all of his belongings, to us, including a white 1966 Mercedes sports convertible with red leather seats. It had been specially designed for him. Sandy flew to New York, packed eight paintings and a few other things from Elie's apartment at the Hotel Pierre in the car, and shipped it back to Los Angeles. (We sold the car shortly thereafter because if anything went wrong with it, we had to order the parts from Germany.) In his will, Elie left both of his apartments to fund student scholarships at Anatolia College in Salonica. He chose Anatolia College because he and his brothers had attended its sister institution, Robert College, in Istanbul.

Love and Marriage

My relationship with Dinos continued to be a strong and loyal friendship on my part, while he was still hoping for a romantic encounter with me that could end up in marriage. He used to talk about our getting married and returning to Greece. My response was always "I can't think of it now, I need to continue with my studies...I do not see marriage in my near future." He was patient with me, concerned about my welfare. He took care of me in every way he could, including lending me money whenever I was short of cash.

After I had been in the States for a year or so, he finished his training and returned to Greece, where he opened his orthodontist's practice in Kolonaki, an elegant neighborhood in Athens. A few years later, he gave up on me and got married. I corresponded with him for a few years after he returned to Greece, and on one of my trips many years later, I visited him at his dental office. It was a warm, sweet reunion. By then, I was married to Sandy and my sons had grown up. After his return to Greece, Dinos had gone to India and had become a devotee of the Maharishi, whose large picture was prominently displayed on the wall of his office. Given my eldest son John's proclivity for seeking a spiritual path as well—at that time John was a devotee of Yogananda—we had a lot to talk about: family, careers, faith, and Dinos' and John's spiritual paths. He told me that his wife had been ill for many years. He was able to deal with it because, he said, "This was my karma." That was my first and last encounter with Dinos since those early years of our relationship, and I thought of him every time we visited Greece. Probably by now he has passed, but I have no way of knowing. I often wished that I had kept our friendship alive. He changed my life in so many ways by helping me come to the U.S.

– * –

Makis was my first love in this country. He was a fellow student at Adelphi, also one of the Lucas' scholarship recipients. He was a year behind me in college, majoring in chemistry. Makis was short, at the most an inch or two taller than I was at five feet, 3.5 inches. He had short, blonde hair that made him look more like a German or Scandinavian—nothing like a Greek man. I admired his brilliant mind and loved the beautifully crafted, poetic letters he wrote to me. He had the gift for creative, vivid, picturesque writing even though he eventually chose a scientific career in chemistry.

I fell in love with him during the end of my first year at Adelphi. We had fun together, studying and playing together, and all the Greek students at Adelphi and in the Lucas group knew of our relationship. There was no question in my mind that he was "the man" in my life. I felt that we were perfectly matched intellectually and emotionally, and I was sure it was going to last for life. We were both very young, only nineteen years old, encountering our first love relationship—so sweet and so special. But a few days before the senior prom, Makis announced to me that he no longer wanted to be in a steady relationship. He felt that he was too young and that he was not ready to make a long-term commitment. I was heartbroken. I cried my eyes out. He was my first real love, not a fantasy like the one I had with Mimis in Greece.

A classmate from Panama, who was a good friend of mine, had made me a beautiful dress for the prom. I managed to get some inexpensive material which she put together to make my first formal dress. It had a white silk top with a pink tulle skirt over a taffeta underskirt. There I was with a fancy dress for the senior prom, without an escort. No Makis in the picture. Mercifully, some friends fixed me up with a blind date, and I did go to the prom, my first such experience. I had fun, but continued to feel devastated over the break with Makis. But time is a healer. I recovered from my break with Makis, and fell in love again with another Greek man.

Demetres was older than Makis by five or six years. He was also in the Lucas group, majoring in engineering. He fascinated me. He had a melancholic look: deep brown eyes with dark circles underneath. He was a widower, always wearing a black tie and his wedding band on his right hand; he carried a lock of his wife's hair in his wallet. As we started to date, he told me about his marriage and his wife's death. He was in love with her before he left Greece. He had come to this country to study with plans to return and marry her. In the meantime, she became ill with leukemia and her parents brought her to the States so that she and Demetres could get married. She could hardly stand straight during the wedding ceremony, and died shortly thereafter. Understandably, he had a difficult time recovering from her death, but this did not bother me. I fell in love with Demetres and I wanted to be with him.

But our relationship lasted less than two years. In 1954, I had gone to the University of Maryland to begin work on my PhD, and he came to visit me. He announced that it was not fair to me continuing in this relationship while he was still in love with his dead wife. He did not say it that way, but in many ways his dead wife was still alive in his life. Again, I felt devastated, and wrote to my parents about my heartbreak. My father was angry that Demetres did that to his "little girl."

I reconnected with Demetres more than thirty years later. He had become a professor at the University of Michigan and I was visiting there for a professional meeting. We had dinner together. It was a welcome reconnection, after all that time, and it gave me closure. He knew that I had obtained my PhD in psychology. He had followed my career by looking at listings and information about me in the American Psychological Association. He also told me that he had had many reoccurring dreams about me. We talked about our families and our professional lives. At one point, he said, "After I retire, I am going back to Greece. I don't want to leave my bones here; I want to be buried back home." That was the last time I saw or heard of Demetres. I am not sure if he is still here or went back to Greece, or if he is dead or alive. That meeting was important to both of us. Even though we both had moved on with our lives, we needed the closure it brought.

At Maryland, I had a most unusual interlude with one of my professors—not exactly sexual. He was an exceptional teacher. One day my earring fell off under the seminar table. He stopped his lecture and stooped under the table to fetch it for me. A few days later, he asked me out to dinner at a fancy restaurant. Fascinated by this invitation, I accepted. The good food, glamorous surroundings, and great conversation were thrilling for a "poor" graduate student, and I loved having the attention from one of my favorite teachers. This curious relationship lasted about a year. He never asked anything of me, never touched me, not even to hold my hand. All he wanted was my presence at occasional dinners and to hear my voice over the telephone. This Dante-esque love interlude abruptly ended the day he heard of my engagement to Sandy.

– * –

Unlike Demetres, Makis had been in and out of my life for a number of years. After he got his B.A., he went to Harvard University for his PhD. I was at the University of Maryland. He decided to reconnect with me and rekindle our relationship. He said that he was still in love with me. I tried to reestablish my feelings of love for him, but it did not work, it did not feel good. I am not sure whether I did not trust him or whether those early romantic feelings could not return. Also, I was still recovering from the breakup with Demetres. Nonetheless, Makis and I continued to try to reestablish our relationship for another year or so, corresponding and visiting occasionally. He stopped writing as soon as he learned that Sandy and I had gotten together.

I saw Makis again in 1976, twenty-two years later, when I went to Michigan State University to give a talk. He was a professor there and had seen the publicity about my visit. I decided to call him, and he invited me to his home for dinner where I met his wife, a Greek-American woman, and his children. After dinner, we sat in the living room. Makis brought out an album of photographs in which there were pictures of the two of us at Adelphi. His wife was present, seemingly unconcerned about his reminiscing about our past relationship, while I sat there with many emotions running through me. The next morning he called to wake me up and drove me to the airport. We promised to remain close and see each other from time to time, and I did see him once or twice in the following two years.

The years I reconnected with Makis were the same years that Sandy and I were having a rough time in our marriage (as I'll discuss later in this book). Perhaps I needed to reexperience those early feelings of falling in love with Makis, to help me to forget the pain I felt from the difficult period with Sandy. I wanted to be validated by Makis, loved by him again as he loved me during my Adelphi University years, and later, when we were both in graduate school.

Before Sandy came into the picture, and while I was still dealing with Demetres and Makis, I developed another romantic relationship with a graduate school classmate, Bernie. Bernie was in love with me, but my feelings toward him were lukewarm. I enjoyed his company and, I must admit, all the attention he gave me, especially the poetry he wrote about me and us. During the summer of 1955, after we started dating, I visited my parents in Greece. It was my first visit since I had left Greece in 1951. By then, my parents had moved to a new apartment they had bought not far from the one we lived in during the war years. I traveled to Greece by boat, a twelve-day voyage each way. I had saved five hundred dollars for this trip, and my parents paid for the return.

Bernie wrote to me often. I told my parents about him, and my mother, somewhat concerned, talked about the possibility of my marrying Bernie, who was Jewish. How would I feel about marrying someone of a different faith and how would I raise the children? I reassured my parents that I had no such plans and that I was going to return home in about a year and a half after finishing my PhD. How little did I know that I was going to start dating Sandy, that I was going to fall deeply in love with him, and that I was going to marry him that coming winter. February 11, 1956, to be exact.

Reflecting on my romantic encounters with men and my falling in love with three young men (Makis, Demetres, Sandy) within a period of three years (1951-1954) makes me feel fickle. How can that be so? In some ways it was inevitable. Even though I was in my late teens and early twenties, I felt more like a teenager, never having dated while growing up in Greece. I liked men, then and now! I am a flirtatious woman, and not particularly aware of my flirtatiousness, something Sandy has told me on numerous occasions.

Throughout those early years of falling in and out of love, I tried to date only Greek men because I was afraid that I might fall in love with an American, which would complicate things since my plan and strong desire was to finish my studies and return to Greece. Regarding Bernie, the first non-Greek man I dated, my excuse was that "I had to finish my studies before I could think about becoming romantically involved with anyone." None of these excuses applied when it came to Sandy, the love of my life, my husband, a fully American man. The same excuses did not apply to him.

Sandy was my classmate at Maryland, extremely tall (six feet five inches), with a fabulous smile with dimples. He wore a crew cut, not a favorite style of mine. He had the look of a typical charming young American man, and he was gregarious, articulate, and creative. We were friends, bumming cigarettes from each other and exchanging class notes for over a year, before we got engaged. I used to give him my tickets for various athletic events. A couple of times he asked me to put up some of his out-of-town girlfriends, which I did, but not always with pleasure, especially when I started to feel romantically inclined toward him. I liked him. I liked his spirit and his many talents, both intellectual and artistic. He courted me by walking me to classes between buildings and often asking if we could stop by the music building. He would say, "I would love to play the piano for you." This was a standard practice of his in trying to court girls, as he told me later: "Girls loved to hear me play the piano."

The day that Sandy asked me for our first date I had a hell of a migraine headache. It was also my last such headache to this day. I had to do everything I could to overcome the headache and go out with Sandy, which I managed to do. I got dressed up, and as I was going out of the apartment to meet Sandy, who was there waiting for me, Bernie arrived carrying some ice cream. He had come over to see me as soon as he heard I was not feeling well. It was an awkward moment for the three of us. At that time, Sandy and Bernie were sharing an office as graduate research assistants. After that first date with Sandy, I told Bernie I was breaking up with him and planning to date Sandy exclusively. He became angry, something I had never seen in him before. Sandy and Bernie had some difficult conversations and it took a long time for the three of us to heal.

My first date with Sandy, on November 18, 1955, turned out to be a memorable experience. First, he arranged for us to go to the Library of Congress where we heard the Budapest String Quartet. After that, he surprised me by taking me to the "Two O'Clock Club," a strip nightclub where I saw the then-famous stripper Blaze Starr do her routine. Blaze Starr was a young woman of twenty-three with raven black hair. She was discreet in her dancing, using flamboyant clothing and a candelabra as her props. (I later learned that she had been the mistress of the governor of Louisiana and that a movie was made about her life, starring Paul Newman.) I had never been to such a club, and to do so on my first date with a man was uncomfortable and embarrassing, to say the least. Sandy later told me that he wanted to show me all different parts of himself right from the beginning—his love for music, which I knew, and his lustful interests.

For our second date, Sandy took me to a jazz nightclub, Club 923. He asked the band to play Jerome Kern's "All the Things You Are." That has been our song over the years. Whenever Sandy and I are out hearing jazz, he always asks the musicians to play this for me. I love it when he does that, because it brings back sweet memories of that second date and our love for jazz. That evening was my introduction to jazz. At first it sounded cacophonous, since the only music I knew and liked was classical. But over the years, I grew to love jazz and it became central to our lives. We have a huge collection; we listen to jazz every Friday evening, if we stay home. Jazz accompanies our cocktail hour, just for the two of us, on Friday, which is our date night whether we go out or stay at home. We have promised each other never to arrange going out with friends on Friday evenings. Our sons and their families and our close friends know about it and never call us on Fridays.

After our second date, Sandy went home and wrote "Lena" in the snow on the roof of his car. His mother later told me he had done this, and that when she saw it, she was convinced that I was "the one" that Sandy was going to marry.

Sandy proposed to me on December 5, 1955, not even a month after our first date, while we were sitting in his old beat-up 1948 black Plymouth. He asked me if I would marry him, and instead of saying "yes," I responded, "When?" He was obviously surprised by my response. Maybe he expected some hesitation on my part, or something more than a one-word "when?" He said, "I need a little time to earn some money so I can buy you a ring." I insisted that I didn't need a ring; I already had one that my mother had given me. Well, we did end up buying rings, our wedding bands, for thirty dollars each, which I proceeded to wear right away. The Greeks wear their wedding bands on their left hand when they get engaged, and on their right hand after they get married. So I followed the Greek tradition. That was the first ring Sandy gave me, but since then he has bought me many others. I have at least ten more rings that he has given me over the years. How little he knew, sitting in that car so long ago, about my love for jewelry!

We got married on February 11, 1956, in Washington D.C. We chose the day because it fell during our break between semesters. We invited everyone we knew—our professors and classmates and other friends. Sandy's parents invited all of their friends. We had about four hundred people at the wedding ceremony at All Souls Unitarian Church, which was officiated by a famous Unitarian minister, A. Powell Davies. Sandy chose the Unitarian Church, where he had attended services for about a year, because it was the only church where he felt comfortable. We arranged to see the minister. When he heard that I was raised Greek Orthodox, he queried me as to whether I would feel comfortable getting married in the Unitarian Church since "Unitarians did not believe that Christ was the son of God," although the church allowed for all sorts of beliefs. This was quite a contradiction as far as I was concerned, but I reassured him that I was fine getting married in the Unitarian Church. Next, we discussed the ceremony and I told him that I wanted to recite St. Paul's epistle on love, one of my favorite passages in the New Testament. I had memorized it in my teens. I wanted to do it and I wanted to recite it in the original, in Greek. He replied that he did not want to have any religious (Christian) elements during the ceremony. I argued with him, saying that this meant a lot to me and how come people can introduce all kinds of personal statements including love songs during the ceremony, but not such a beautiful statement about "Agape"? He would not be persuaded by my arguments, so I let it go. But I have not forgotten it. I proposed to Sandy that we get married in the Greek Orthodox Church, but he said that he would feel uncomfortable not knowing the language and saying "yes" to things he did not understand. Being eager to have the wedding ceremony, I decided that it was not worth arguing about with Sandy and the minister of the Unitarian Church. Our wedding and the ceremony at the All Souls Unitarian Church took place on that rainy Saturday of February 11.

Greece, however, did not recognize a marriage if it was performed outside the Greek Orthodox tradition. So my Greek godfather, uncle

Euripides, arranged for us to get married in the church during one of our visits to Greece. The boys, now eight and ten, were excited and intrigued by the idea, and they told all the kids in the neighborhood, "My parents are going to get married when we go to Greece." It must have made quite an impression on their friends and their friends' parents, but no one said anything to us. Unfortunately, the Greek wedding never happened, to my disappointment and to that of my Greek relatives. Sandy continued to feel uncomfortable about the idea of a Greek wedding.

Sandy's parents held the wedding reception at their home for 150 of their closest friends and relatives. The Cosmos Club catered the event and a photographer took twelve pictures, which was all we could afford in those days. To my delight, my brother came. Two friends were my bridesmaids–Margaret, my graduate school roommate, and Artemis. Uncle Elie was pleased when I asked him to be my "surrogate father" for the wedding and give me away. He charmed every woman he met, young and old, kissing their hand and complimenting each one of them. They all talked about him for months afterward, about how charming and continental he was.

My parents were not able to come to the wedding, but they sent me a bouquet of my favorite carnations. I carried that bouquet everywhere–to the place I stayed the night before the wedding and on our honeymoon. It represented a touch of my parents. Our honeymoon lasted just a few days and we spent it at an inexpensive motel in the nearby city of Baltimore. We were a poor young couple—just graduate students, madly in love. After our short honeymoon, we came back to our small apartment in College Park near the campus of the University of Maryland. We managed to furnish it with secondhand furniture. But our upright piano, our one and only luxury, dominated the living room.

I became close to Sandy's parents, who lived about half an hour away from our apartment. Sandy's mother Margaret always said that I was the daughter she never had. She had only two boys: Sandy and his older brother John. Margaret, or Mom, as I addressed her, married Sandy's father (Pop) when they were both undergraduates at the University of Utah. Both were born and raised in Utah. Pop was mostly of English heritage while Mom's family was somewhat English and Irish but mostly Scottish. Pop had lost his father when he was six and assumed a lot of responsibility at an early age. Mom came from a rather well-to-do family. Her father was an engineer and businessman; her mother had been a soloist with the Mormon Tabernacle choir. Her parents eventually divorced.

Pop was raised as a Mormon and had contemplated a mission trip when Mom insisted that he give up his Mormon faith if the two were to get engaged. He did; they got married and left Utah for New York where they pursued graduate education. Pop became a well-known physicist, and for seventeen years directed the National Bureau of Standards, a Presidential appointment. Mom had a brief career in journalism before she started the family. She always regretted not doing more with her intellectual and career interests. There was a sadness to her, and I think she felt frustrated not having a life of her own. She was an entertaining storyteller, but also a complicated woman who often expressed her own insecurities in personal attacks toward the very members of her family she loved dearly.

Mom could not do enough for me. She was an excellent seamstress and took it upon herself to sew for me; some of the most elegant clothes I had those days as a graduate student were made by her. She loved to get designer patterns and beautiful fabrics for the outfits she sewed for me, her "little girl." While we were at the University of Maryland, Sandy and I spent every Sunday with them. They loved to feed and take care of those two "starving" graduate students. A delicious roast beef with mashed potatoes and peas was the standard menu, with one of Mom's pies for dessert. I recollect those Sunday meals and visits with such fondness. The folks, as we referred to them, not only fed and took care of us, but they also read every page of our dissertations and gave us astute feedback on our work. It amazed me that Pop, the hardcore physicist, read my dissertation on empathy and not only gave me good feedback, but also enjoyed it.

Sandy's parents became my American parents. His father was similar to mine, a loving, quiet man. He was proud of my accomplishments, but as a man of his times, he was unsure about my working while I was also trying to raise young children. He had been president of the Cosmos Club in Washington and he did not see anything wrong with the club's practices of not allowing women to be members or even to enter through the front door. We had many an argument about it. Those days, the exclusive club, created by men for men, selected its members based on their professional achievements. Women not only could not become members, but women guests were relegated to a lower status by being treated like hired help. Pop could not see anything wrong with this and would argue with me that "men need to have a place of their own where they can get together without interference by women."

As I became a stronger and more outspoken feminist, I refused to participate with the family at those occasional dinners at the Cosmos Club. Sandy accepted an invitation to join the club, expecting that the club's bylaws would soon change to admit women. When his petition was voted down—because he was perceived as a "troublemaker"— Sandy resigned and sent the club a strongly worded letter of protest. Many years later, when women were finally admitted as members, my boss at UCLA, Provost Ray Orbach, wanted to nominate me for membership. I had achieved visibility in my profession by then, and indeed, was serving as Associate Provost with him. But given my history with the Cosmos Club and its discrimination against women, I had no interest in being recognized for membership in a formerly sexist elite club.

After we moved to Los Angeles, Sandy's parents visited us often. When Pop passed away, Mom moved here permanently, to an apartment about fifteen minutes away from us. She enjoyed our frequent visits and spent holiday dinners and parties with us and our friends. Then, tragically, she died in a terrible accident. While alone in her apartment, her cigarette started a fire in her armchair. She suffered burns all over her body before she could be transported to a burn center, and lived for three days before she passed. I was the only one in the room when she took her last breath. I became angry at the nurse who was trying to redirect some of the lines of equipment that kept her alive. My pain was so intense, seeing the monitor cease to show any signs of life, that I lashed out at the poor nurse for causing Mom's death.

Mom had a rocking chair in her apartment where I would sit every time we visited her. The chair got terribly burned during the fire. But I managed to rescue it and refinish it, and that chair now resides in our house in Malibu. It reminds me of Mom, and our love for each other.

Maternal ancestor
Yannis Boukouvalas,
a warrior (1700s)

*From National Historic
Museum of Greece*

Maternal ancestor
Yannakis Boukouvalas,
a warrior (1700s)

*From National Historic
Museum of Greece*

John and Eleni
Boukouvala,
maternal
grandparents

Family portrait,
1933

Lena (lower center) with brother Alex (upper left) and four cousins

Age six with Mother and Alex, 1938

With Cousin
Costas, 1937

My wartime doll Erini
("Peace"), Athens, 1940

High school
graduation, 1949

Junior year at
Adelphi University,
1951–1952

Playing Debussy,
Adelphi University,
1952

Just married (1956), All Souls Unitarian Church, Washington, D.C.

Sandy's parents, Margaret and Allen Astin, 1957

With Alex,
Lexington, KY, 1957

My parents with cousin Ioanna, Salonica, Greece, 1957

With cousin Ioanna,
during my first visit
with Sandy to
Greece, 1958

At age twenty-eight,
Baltimore, M.D., 1960

Mother reading
Dr. Seuss' *The Cat in
the Hat* to the boys
during her first visit
to the U.S. (1963)

CHAPTER 3

A Budding Psychologist

While attending Adelphi University (1951–1953), I majored in psychology, enjoying every course I took. I had always been interested in psychology, even before I came to the U.S. I had a strong curiosity about people, the intricacies of human life, of being—the great questions of what makes us who we are and the choices we make in our lives. Both in Greece and here, I was intrigued with the question of how people choose their life's work. So it is not surprising that my honor's thesis at Adelphi was about how college women choose their majors, and the role the family plays in shaping these choices. The psychology of gender and, in particular, the educational and career development of women, was of great interest to me early on in my academic career and has remained a central theme in my research and writing throughout my professional career.

While attending Adelphi, I went to visit the dean of the graduate division to get some guidance from her about what I should do next, what program of study to pursue in graduate school, and where. She was a professor of Spanish as well as the dean. I told her that I was interested in working with people, but that I was also interested in doing research about people, and that I was driven by a passion for inquiry. She looked at me, puzzled, and proceeded to tell me that she did not believe that I could do both. "Either you are a clinical psychologist, or you are a researcher," she said. "You can't combine both interests."

In spite of these discouraging and somewhat confusing, if not erroneous, words, I decided to go ahead and apply to graduate school for my Master's degree. Mr. Lucas suggested a couple of colleges with graduate programs that could be suitable: Smith College and Bryn Mawr College. I had never heard of either of them; for that matter, I was completely ignorant about differences among colleges based on their resources and reputations. But when I saw that there was a college in Athens, Ohio—Ohio University—I announced, "I am going to go to Athens, to Ohio University. There might be some Greek students there." I spent a year and a half at Ohio University, and indeed, there were some Greek students there. I earned my Master's in psychology there, mentored by Dr. James Patrick, a most supportive advisor. For my thesis, I chose a rather complicated topic: a study of the process of acculturation of foreign students and the role psychological well-being played in it. Dr. Patrick discouraged me from choosing such an involved topic for a master's thesis, but that did not stop me.

In many ways, it was a study of "mesearch." As a student from another country and culture, I tried to understand the process of acculturation and adjustment. Those days I was very much into Freud's writings, so I decided to study "identification," an important Freudian construct. I was curious to learn how students' ability to identify with aspects of their own culture transfer to a new culture, and how their mental health mediates the transition to the new culture and their assimilation into it. The study revealed that students' readiness to migrate to another country and their ability to identify with aspects of the new culture were critical factors in how well they were able to assimilate into the new country. Their mental health, as I measured it, did not appear to play a role in their assimilation.

The psychological measure I used was the Sentence Completion Test. In completing one of the sentences that began, "I hope . . . ," one of my student subjects wrote: ". . . the Indians will win." I immediately went to Dr. Patrick, concerned about the mental health of anyone who had such a fantasy about Indians, all along thinking of American Indians. I had no idea that it stood for a sports' team, the Cleveland Indians. I had a long way to go in getting acculturated!

My knowledge of sports teams remains dismal to this day. Some time ago, I was at a meeting of the advisory board of the Genesee Center, a shelter for abused women in south Los Angeles. Other board members were talking about the generous contribution of furniture to the Center made by someone named Magic Johnson. In total innocence I said, "Who is Magic Johnson?" A heresy indeed, especially in Los Angeles. Everyone else knew who Magic Johnson was: a famous basketball player, Ervin Johnson, who was, and continues to be, a local and national celebrity. I was plenty embarrassed when I saw my colleagues' looks in response to my question. And I learned my lesson fast: Do not ask "Who is this person?" Just go home and find out on your own.

At Ohio, I met other Greek students, and, of course, we became good friends. The Greek men organized themselves into a soccer team and they asked me and another Greek student, Anna, to cheerlead for them. I did not know anything about soccer, but I knew how to cheer whenever our team scored a goal. We went to local dances.

It was the era of Glenn Miller—great music, great slow dancing. George, an engineering student, became my part-time boyfriend. He had an American girlfriend who lived in Columbus. He was committed to her, but I did not mind his attention and we dated whenever he was around Athens. We had fun times together. Anna would often come along with another male Greek student as her date. Neither Anna nor I was interested in serious dating, but we loved the male attention and had fun going to the movies, dancing, and, of course, cheering the guys at the soccer games.

My life at Ohio University was very different from the two years I spent at Adelphi. By the time I got to Athens, I felt comfortable with English, I was much more assimilated into American culture, and, of course, I had become confident of my academic abilities. I had male attention without the ups and downs of being in love. I continued with my music by finding a devoted piano teacher who loved teaching me because I was doing it out of love for the piano; studying piano was not a required course for the major. He even taught me for free although I was a private student and not in the program. In appreciation for his kindness, I asked my mother to send him a beautiful art object from Greece, and she did—a Greek vase. He was delighted to receive it and, of course, I was happy that I was able to reciprocate.

Besides teaching me, my piano teacher enjoyed hearing anecdotes about my experiences as a student in psychology. Some were more harrowing than others. In one of my classes, we were told that a then-famous psychiatrist, Walter Freeman, was going to perform lobotomies at the nearby state hospital, and that we could go and observe. I jumped at the opportunity. On the day I went, Dr. Freeman told us that he had just performed his twelve hundredth lobotomy. (He would go on to do more than five thousand of them.) In those days, lobotomies could be disastrous for patients. I stood a few feet away and watched. Dr. Freeman first used electroshock to anesthetize the patient, then inserted two ice picks through the eye sockets, where they were used to slice through the patient's frontal lobes. Thus the name of the procedure – transorbital lobotomy. The most unthinkable part of the surgeries that I witnessed that day was when Freeman asked an untrained doctor, perhaps a medical resident, to perform one of the lobotomies. As the resident cut into the patient's lobes with the ice picks, Freeman said to him, "No, no, take them out, reinsert them, keep a larger angle between the picks, and try again." I remember thinking, "I can't believe they are cutting into this person's frontal lobes so blindly." I wondered how the poor patient would function after this brutal procedure, cognitively and emotionally. I did not stay around long enough to see the effects of this surgery on the patients I observed. But I read later about the success rate. It was minimal.

Finishing my day at the state hospital, I went straight to my piano lesson where I described the gruesome details of how lobotomies were done. I always wondered why he, an artist, was so interested. Either I was a good storyteller or he had some special interest in psychiatry.

Working on My PhD

As I was completing the work for my Master's degree, my advisor said, "Lena, since you are here in this country, why don't you get your PhD before you go back home?" Thinking that his advice made sense, I applied to a number of schools that he recommended. He also advised me to enter the field of counseling psychology rather than clinical psychology. When I returned to Greece, he said, my training in counseling psychology would provide more work opportunities than would clinical training, which would put me in competition with psychiatrists. I applied to five graduate programs and chose the University of Maryland because their acceptance letter was the warmest and most welcoming.

I arrived at the University of Maryland at the end of the summer of 1954. In my letter of acceptance, I was offered only one half of an assistantship. But when I met with the chair of the department, I asked him if he could provide me with another half, since I did not have any other resources and I would not be able to survive on six hundred dollars per year. He immediately made a couple of phone calls and offered me another half of an assistantship. Having twelve hundred dollars for the year was enough to cover my living and school expenses—another omen that Maryland was to be the place for me, and that the faculty and administration were going to look out for me.

During my first three years in the program, I roomed with other women graduate students, which helped reduce the overall costs of room and board. The psychology graduate program at the University of Maryland was small—only thirty-two students in the Master's and PhD combined. Besides me, there were only two other women going for their PhDs, and I was the second woman in the history of the department to earn that advanced degree. In those days we were rare indeed. In 1957, the year I graduated, across all fields there were only a thousand women in the entire country who received PhDs, compared to 7,200 men.

My three years at the University of Maryland were memorable— and not only because I met and married Sandy there. We had an excellent group of faculty and interesting courses. My advisor, Dr. Jack Gustad, and other faculty were some of the best teachers and mentors I encountered during the six years I spent in three different American universities. I did not feel any overt gender discrimination with the exception of one episode when I was deciding about my two specializations for the PhD. My primary one was counseling psychology.

For the second, I wanted to major in statistics. Dr. Gustad discouraged me because, he said, statistics was not an appropriate specialization for women. He advised me to choose social psychology, which I did. However, wanting to prove him wrong, I took every statistics course that was offered in the program, and I did well in each one of them. I made my point that gender should not be considered in educational advising.

I did my dissertation on empathy. I developed a situational test of empathy, by measuring the degree of empathy exhibited by therapists in a simulated therapeutic encounter. I selected actual client statements from transcribed therapeutic sessions. My brother-in-law, John Astin, a professional actor, playacted each statement as though it were being spoken by a person in therapy. Students who were in training as counseling psychologists were my research subjects. They were asked to listen to each of the ten recorded statements and respond as a therapist might have done. I recorded their responses. In turn, a set of experienced clinical psychologists were asked to judge the amount of empathy exhibited by each of my subjects in how they responded to the client's statement.

Comparing my situational approach to measuring empathy to a paper-and-pencil approach proved that the situational test had greater potential for tapping into a person's empathic ability more accurately. However, other than publishing a single article on this research, I never did any further work on empathy, although it was a hot topic in those days and my approach to assessing empathy offered some promise.

Sandy and I developed many common intellectual interests, which played a role in how our career lives have evolved over time. During those years at Maryland, we took the PhD exams and wrote our dissertations at the same time. However, we approached our intellectual endeavors differently and had different styles of studying and writing. I have always tried to do my work without any distractions. When I work I like to shut myself in my study with the door closed and focus on what I'm doing in absolute quiet. Sandy, on the other hand, likes to be in the midst of a lot of other activity while he works. He will be in the living room listening to a football game on the radio while doing his studying or writing. That is how he works to this day—hardly ever using his study. One summer on Cape Cod, we were vacationing with another family of good friends, living in the same house—four adults and four children (ages one and a half to five). Sandy worked on one of his books while sitting in the living room and dictating. The four kids would be running around making all kinds of noise, including the eighteen-month-old baby who would stand by Sandy banging on a metal coffee table. I guess she was keeping time with Sandy's dictation.

Our graduate school days were the start of a professional colleagueship that has lasted to this day. While studying for the PhD qualifying exams, we borrowed each other's notes for courses we had not taken. We studied separately, but we had many discussions on the materials we read.

In those days, graduate students were required to demonstrate fluency in two languages. French was easy for us; we both had had enough French as undergraduates to pass the exam easily. But German was another matter. Neither of us had any knowledge of German, but we needed to learn enough to be able to translate a passage from a psychology text, using a dictionary to help. That exercise of using the dictionary while trying to comprehend something in another, unknown language brought back memories of my earlier struggles with English, and filled me with anxiety and apprehension all over again.

We hired a German graduate student to help us prepare. He behaved like a stereotypical German. During the lessons, he would pace back and forth in our tiny living room and command us to respond to his questions using our limited German vocabulary. He had no sense of humor and never praised us if we did well. I did not feel anxious or fearful of him, in spite of my early experiences with Germans during the occupation, but I could not relate to him because he was so stiff and cold in his demeanor. Sandy and I decided to work on our own, primarily by trying to memorize as many words as we could. We thought that would help us to spend less of the allotted exam time looking up words. When we took the exams, I passed but Sandy had to take it again. Even though what he translated was perfect, he did not translate enough of the passage because he had not memorized enough words.

Our social life was mostly with the other graduate students. We would have dinners and parties at each others' apartments, bringing food and drink. Brian Shepp, a classmate, and his wife June lived a few doors down from us. June was working full-time so they were financially in much better shape than the rest of us. They owned a TV set and we spent many evenings with them watching their little screen, hooked on Alfred Hitchcock and Jonathan Winters. The other big form of entertainment was going to outdoor movie theaters, the drive-ins.

The most traumatic experience for me in graduate school was the qualifying exams. I was not alone; we all felt a generalized anxiety about them. One of our classmates, an excellent student, went into panic mode and started to fantasize about stealing the exam questions. His anxiety eventually made him physically sick and he had to postpone taking the exams. I also was so nervous that I kept vomiting the morning of the exam, both at home and at school. But I managed to get through it and pass, which gave me the honor of becoming a candidate for the PhD. And all that was left was the dissertation, which I did easily and with pleasure.

First Job

Sandy and I got our PhDs in the summer of 1957, at age twenty-five, and moved to Lexington, Kentucky, for our first jobs. At that time, Lexington housed the only federal penitentiary for drug addiction. The place doubled as a hospital for the treatment of the drug addicts who came in either as "volunteers" or as Federal prisoners who were required to serve time for nonviolent crimes, primarily selling drugs or other offenses committed to support their habit. Most of the women had been arrested for prostitution, but they were serving time for other petty crimes like stealing and forgery. The hospital also had a unit that treated people serving in the Coast Guard or Merchant Marines who had psychiatric disorders.

Sandy was hired as a commissioned officer in the Public Health Service to satisfy his two years of required service. I was hired as a civilian clinical psychologist. During our two years in Lexington, we were involved in diagnostic work and in treatment of the inmates. We did both individual and group psychotherapy. Since the hospital also had a research unit, Sandy engaged in research as well and managed to publish a few articles. The population we worked with were truly hardcore drug addicts. The drug of choice those days was heroin. The patients came from all socioeconomic levels and included a few doctors and nurses, most of whom used prescription drugs.

This was the hardest professional work I have ever done. It was emotionally draining. I had never before dealt with people who had so much intelligence and artistic talent while at the same time being so troubled psychologically. Our patients lived lives that were not part of my experience. In my training, I had dealt with neurotic and psychotic patients but had never encountered persons with sociopathic tendencies and disorders. While there, I treated a patient who talked about how he used to steal merchandise from Marshall Fields, one of Chicago's oldest and most upscale department stores. He would put on a large overcoat and stuff it with stolen cashmere sweaters. He felt no guilt, he said, about any of the stolen goods, because he believed that the store could cover its losses with insurance. That was the most common rationalization our patients provided for their petty crimes.

During our time in Lexington, I became pregnant with our first son. One day a huge, beautifully packaged box arrived from Neiman Marcus, in Houston. Puzzled, since I did not know anyone who lived there, I opened the box and found the most beautiful baby clothes. I laid them all on the bed, admiring them, and I started to cry with joy, excited in anticipation of my first child while still wondering who had sent me this beautiful bundle of clothing. In the bottom of the box was a sweet note from one of my former patients. When she returned to the hospital, re-addicted, I went up to her and said, "Mary, you should not have done this, spending all this money." She looked at me, and with a smile said, "Honey, don't you worry about it. I forged a check."

Treatments in those days were ineffective. The protocol was: help inmates to withdraw from physical dependence, provide them with some psychotherapy, and release them. Most of the patients I worked with either came back re-addicted or died on the streets from an overdose. After they were released, most if not all of our patients returned back to the same environment, same neighborhood, and same friends. It was inevitable that they would resume the same behavioral patterns and habits. Many of the patients who came to the hospital as volunteers were mostly motivated by the need to withdraw, so that when they returned back home after treatment their habit would not require as much of the drug for them to get high. Some of the patients admitted hiding their drug paraphernalia by the gate of the hospital before they came in for treatment. That way, they would have them handy when they hit the streets again. Many times, I thought of leaving my job and looking for something more uplifting, less disappointing or depressing, but I decided to remain with it as I started to adapt, understand, and even accept the pathology of the people I was working with.

I had treated a young man in therapy who fell in love with one of the women patients there. Even though they kept the women and men apart, the patients found plenty of ways to make contact. If they happened to be in group therapy together, they would pass "kites" (as they called short notes) to each other or to someone who could give it to another inmate when they got back to their living quarters. The religious services were fertile ground for exchanges between the sexes. Besides the exchange of kites during the service, they would also exchange sexual touches with the person of the opposite sex sitting next to them.

When one of my patients and his woman left the hospital, they decided to set up house in Lexington. I continued to see him on an outpatient basis. I was delighted that they made the decision to stay in Lexington and not return to their hometown and old neighborhood. That helped them to abstain from drugs for awhile. One day he told me how they made their livelihood. He found the "johns" who would be serviced by his girlfriend, while he would visit the horse races to pick some pockets. If there was money in the wallet he stole, he would behave "honorably," removing the money and putting the empty wallet in the mailbox so that it could be returned to its owner. If there was no money, he threw the wallet into the closest garbage can. And yet their criminal behavior did not particularly upset me.

My own thinking had become twisted. I was happy that they had managed to stay clean.

I worked hard with my patients, trying to help them change, but continued to feel like a failure, while in the meantime recognizing that they appreciated that I cared about them. Their welfare was paramount in my mind. I was able to develop good relationships with them, and I believe I was important in their lives. A number of them corresponded with me after they left Lexington, reaching out and wanting to relate to me. Perhaps they were looking for my support and approval. In many ways, this particular patient population is very needy for approval.

For a while, I had worked with a renowned jazz musician, a talented composer. He would come to our session bringing his records, which he wanted me to take home and listen to. It was a genuine gesture of wanting to share something he was proud of–his achievement as a composer of jazz tunes that have become classics. His music is still played often in jazz clubs, and every time I hear it I think of him, hoping I helped him in some ways. I can't say, because he had a hard time accepting the therapeutic encounter. He would come to the session, but not even get completely inside my office. He would put his chair halfway in my office with the other half out in the hallway. He could not open up about anything personal, but he would share the music he had composed and recorded.

There was pain and richness in my life during those two years in Lexington. There was pain from working with clients who were so psychologically damaged and from feeling that I could do so little for them. I can hardly count a patient or two that I was able to help overcome his or her addiction. I was only twenty-five, and this was my first professional job, but still, I felt like a failure. While my supervisor kept assuring me that I was well-trained and talented and doing a good job, it was I who felt inadequate, not seeing any positive outcomes or impact from my work with my patients.

But there was also a lot of richness in my life that came from the lasting friendships we had developed in Lexington. While there, we met and became friends with two young psychiatrists who were like brothers to us: Bob Osnos and Jack Mead. They, along with their wives, have remained among our closest friends over the years. We have continued to take yearly vacations with them, and our adult children remain connected to their children.

Lexington was a small town in those days. When we first got there, Sandy and I were the only married couple, but soon after we arrived, Bob and Jack followed in our footsteps and got married as well. Naomi, Bob's wife, had her first child Gwyn just a week after our son John was born. We had the same ob-gyn doctor, and welcomed each other's firstborns right at the hospital. It has been a strong friendship among all six of us. We have celebrated special occasions together and shared each other's griefs and illnesses.

My first job in Lexington taught me about myself as well: How difficult it is for me not to meet my professional expectations; how not to give up; how to persist and learn whatever I can from any experience. Lexington helped me hone my psychotherapeutic skills and cultivate my empathic abilities, which continue to come in handy no matter what the setting or the people involved in any of my jobs since.

Balancing Work and Family

Our first son, John, was born in Lexington on August 28, 1959. Three weeks later, we moved to Baltimore, MD, where Sandy had been offered a job as a research psychologist at a Veteran's Administration hospital. After a few months of getting settled and taking care of my newborn, I decided to go back to work. I knew that I would be a happier person and a better mother and wife if I were engaged in professional work. I found work part-time as an instructor in pediatrics at a clinic for epileptic children at the University of Maryland Medical Center. The job required my doing psychological diagnostic work with the children and interpreting the results for medical residents, parents, and teachers. Sandy was unhappy at his new job, however, and decided to look for another as soon as he could, so before spending even a year in Baltimore, we moved again.

Sandy's next job was in Chicago, at the National Merit Scholarship Corporation, doing educational research. By the time we moved there, in August 1960, I had become pregnant again with our second son, Paul, who was born in Evanston, a suburb of Chicago, on March 2, 1961. I waited a few months and then found a job as a faculty member in psychology at the nearby National College of Education, the oldest private teachers' college in the United States. I spent four happy years teaching there. The school was only ten minutes away from where we lived so I could go home in between classes if any of the kids got sick. The registrar at the college was accommodating, scheduling my classes at time slots that were best for me, so I would teach twice a week in the morning and be home for most of the day.

While I was engaged and happy in my professional life, I started to feel the dilemmas and pressures of trying to balance work with the demands of motherhood. Among our friends and Sandy's professional colleagues, I was the only working mother. I did not feel resentment from women friends, but I felt it from Sandy's colleagues, who believed that Sandy's career might suffer since he had to take over some of the load in managing the household chores. His boss, who was also a good friend of mine, used to say, "Sandy, you can go to the moon if you were to stay longer in the office and not worry about Lena and the kids so much." How I used to resent this kind of talk and the boss's dismissal of my professional interests and achievements! I felt some disapproval from Sandy's mother—not overt, but it was there. On the other hand, my mother was supportive, and she was even unhappy that I had stopped working for almost a year before I gave birth to Paul.

Finding adequate child care was one of my most anxiety-producing tasks. I felt I had to accommodate to the quirks of my child care providers as long as they cared lovingly for my children's needs. When I returned to full-time work, I decided to hire someone who could live with us and help with the children. That way, the helper would be there when I needed to go to school and not worry whether or not the babysitter would show up. There is no flexibility when you have a class full of students; you can't call and say, "Sorry, but I have a sick kid at home, and my babysitter did not show up." You have to be there to teach your class.

Evanston was a happy time for us. The kids were growing up and getting out of diapers. I registered them in the preschool program at the Lab School of the teacher's college where I was teaching. The Lab School had a great reputation, and it was a relief to have both boys in classrooms next to my own class where I was teaching child development. While this was not my field, it certainly fit my life, as I was raising two young children. I also taught "Guidance in the Elementary School" and served as the college's counselor for students with academic and personal problems and concerns. John was about two when he decided to sit next to me with paper and pencil in hand while I was preparing my notes for class. He would say, "I am doing my work, too."

John started in nursery school as he turned three. He insisted on going to school on the bus. He chose his own clothing and most of the time he got dressed up as though he were going to a party. Often, mothers would call me to ask me if there was a special event at school because "Johnnie Astin came to school all dressed up." And I would think, "There goes my son, a future dandy." He was the first one to be picked up by the bus and he would ride for forty-five minutes instead of the ten to fifteen minutes that it would take me to drive him. But the bus appealed to him. Was he declaring his independence at age three, or was he just enjoying the ride, the various stops, and seeing the different neighborhoods? I think it was both.

Paul was a different story. He did not want to go to school; for days he would cry after I dropped him off and left him. I was surprised, because I was practically next door to him and his brother was also there. Paul and his crying made him a cause célèbre. Mothers would come by to tell me that "he cried much less today."

I wasn't sure why Paul was that uncomfortable about school. I suspected that his vivid imagination might have made him apprehensive at being in a new place. Nonetheless, his discomfort made me anxious and uncertain about what I should do. Ultimately, I kept him in school and tried to reassure him that he would be okay and that I was there, right next door to him. He continued to be fearful. One day the school psychologist invited him to her room to be tested. She said to Paul, "Come in, and we can play some games." He replied, "My brother does not play with you." But eventually, he trusted her enough to go into her office and be tested. She gave him an IQ test, on which he did very well.

In spite of Paul's difficult beginning school days, both kids ended up having great experiences in the lab school and all the notes I got from their teachers were positive. Their (different) teachers described them as "delightful children," telling us how impressed they were with the boys' caring attitude toward other children and their willingness to help other children, especially little girls, who were shy or awkward. This pleased me.

Our first live-in babysitter, who was in her forties, left while we were still living in Evanston, so we decided to hire as our next nanny a young girl of eighteen or nineteen from the farm country in nearby Green Bay, Wisconsin. We had two such nannies in consecutive years. Pat, a robust country girl, stayed for a year but became homesick and returned back to her family in Wisconsin. Jacki, the second, came to us in 1964 and stayed for five years. She was nineteen, attractive with blonde-red hair, and liked to dress fashionably. She became part of our family. She had an artistic flair and loved to do all kinds of art projects with the boys. Paul was her favorite and they became close. She came to Washington with us after we left Evanston and to Palo Alto for the year (1967–68) we spent there. When we came back to Washington, the boys were older and needed less attention, so Jacki took courses at the University of Maryland and eventually returned home. We kept in touch with Jacki, and to this day exchange emails, while the boys are on Facebook with her. She finished college, has had a successful business career, got married, divorced, and had three children of her own—all grown up now.

In Evanston, we purchased our first house, a colonial across from a park. It was my dream house. It had enough space for all our needs, including a great finished basement where the kids and their friends spent most of their time during those freezing winter days in Chicago. Finished basements are a necessity in cold climates. Social life in Chicago meant getting together with friends to share a meal, have lively conversation, or play a game of bridge. Most summers, we stayed around Chicago, since we had beautiful Lake Michigan in our backyard, a perfect place for swimming and sunning on the beach. Bob and Naomi Osnos and their children spent a summer with us vacationing by Lake Michigan.

– * –

As I reflect back on those years, I have come to realize how atypical my life was compared to many of the neighborhood women and our circle of friends. I was a full-time mom; I was the one who took care of all the household needs, shopping, cooking, and entertaining. Although I carried a large burden in trying to combine full-time work and raising two young children, I do not remember feeling any resentment then. Mostly, I felt overwhelmed, especially during our various moves. Each move meant locating the right new doctors and schools for the children and finding adequate household help and babysitters. That was fine with me; I felt that Sandy's career took precedence over mine. My work was just work; I was not pursuing a career.

Yet I was doing interesting work that allowed me to use my skills and training as a psychologist. I was supported by my colleagues and did not feel any gender discrimination. Since there were few professional women in the workplace during the late fifties and early sixties, we professional women did not represent a threat that we could possibly take over the men's positions. Moreover, the labor market was much more robust in those days; plenty of jobs were available for highly educated men and women. Sandy had no problems with my working; he was happy to see me intellectually engaged and satisfied, and that has been true during our entire life as a married couple. He always has been proud of my accomplishments. Perhaps the fact that his mother was unhappy and frustrated for not having pursued her passion for journalism might have played a role in his supporting my need to pursue my professional interests and stay in the workforce.

Still, looking back, I recognize how often we moved and what that meant for me, my work, and all the issues surrounding our family life. We didn't have much discussion about whether we should move or not, either. Sandy made the choice of the next job, and I went along.

Sandy was a young man going to the moon, after all, so he was being recruited actively; he was being pursued and I followed. Eventually, that pattern took its toll on me. While I was not consciously upset at the time—I had accepted the stereotypical view that a man's career comes first—the many moves took an emotional toll.

Sandy had little patience with my agonizing about the issues I was facing trying to get settled after each move. He would say, "Why are you so preoccupied with the nanny thing, who is going to be the nanny, and how you are going to get a nanny? Why are you making such a big deal of it?" And I would respond, "Because I cannot do what I would like to do workwise until I take care of all these matters."

If I were a professional woman today, I believe that I would do things differently. I would insist that I find work that interested and pleased me before my partner and I moved anywhere. And we would negotiate more clearly who is responsible for household chores and child care. In my day, we were not as conscious about the importance of these issues as today's dual-career families are. But as time went on, Sandy became much more present as a father, especially as the boys were getting older, and played a greater part in child rearing. Whether that was because I asked for more help as I got more involved with my own career, or whether he recognized the need on his own, I am not sure. It just happened. We evolved into much more of an egalitarian partnership as time went on.

When I see now how recent generations of women and men negotiate career and family tasks and responsibilities, I regret that my generation took it for granted that the wife's career had to take second place to that of her husband's. But I do recognize that, for those times, it was the thing to do.

CHAPTER 4

Family Ties

My life has been enormously enriched by my sons and their families. My sons, now in their fifties, are two of the most interesting and caring people I know. I like being around them. The two are very different from each other, which enriches my life even more.

John, my oldest, has had a unique and uneven life trajectory. As a teenager, he was the easy one. A good student, he managed to spend a great deal of time around the house with his friends, often playing their favorite game of poker. He was popular at school and socially and politically aware. He chose the University of California at Berkeley as his university to attend because, in his mind, that was a place with activist students he'd have a lot in common with. He planned to study political science and change the world.

During his first year at Berkeley, 1977, John was actively engaged in student leadership roles. He participated in student protests and almost got jailed for it. He finished his first year successfully, but during the summer months something happened. He no longer saw meaning in what he was doing and announced to us that he was not going to continue his studies at Berkeley. To our amazement and great disappointment, he decided to drop out of college, just at the time Sandy published his book, *Preventing Students from Dropping Out*. We could not figure out the meaning of John's act of "dropping out." Was it a coincidence with the publication of Sandy's book, or was it a statement of his need to be different from his parents and in claiming his independence from us?

For the next year he lived on Telegraph Avenue in Berkeley. He worked at a pizza place to earn his livelihood, and experimented with drugs, including LSD. It was a tough year for us; we had to figure out how to maintain our relationship with him and accept his new lifestyle and behavior, so different from what we had come to expect from him. We decided that all we could do was to keep being present in his life, and that the best thing was to go up there as often as we could to visit him, keeping the channels of communication open. But he showed no interest in our visiting nor in our being there. He would join some of his buddies and beat drums for long periods in front of Sproul Hall, the administration building at Berkeley—keeping his unkempt hair long, wearing clothes from the Salvation Army, and being uncommunicative, just in his own world, beating the drums.

John lived that way for a year, at which time he decided to attend UC Santa Cruz, since we had told him that we would support him financially only if he were attending college. So, with little motivation for college, he transferred to Santa Cruz, where he took pottery and modern dance, continuing his journey of searching for who he was and what life was about. In the process of searching, John came upon the *Autobiography of a Yogi* by Yogananda, an Indian yogi and guru who had founded an organization called the Self-Realization

Fellowship in the United States. Reading that book moved John into a transformational journey. He started to meditate for hours at a time. He became a true yogi, a total Yogananda devotee, and considered joining the Self-Realization Fellowship's order of brothers-monks. My heart broke. I felt that I was going to lose my son to a movement that was alien to me. When I read the Fellowship's literature on becoming a monk, it indicated that he could not see or communicate with his family for at least eighteen months. The idea of not being able to see him or be with him was difficult to accept. At the same time, he considered returning and finishing college before making a final decision to join the order of Brothers.

At my suggestion, John applied and got accepted to Hampshire College, in Amherst, Massachusetts. I had served as a trustee of Hampshire College and felt that their curriculum and the way they had structured the academic experience would be perfect for him. At Hampshire, he could be self-directed and follow his intellectual passions, which he did. He spent two years there completing his work for his Bachelor's degree. His senior thesis was an examination of the relationship between Eastern and Western psychological constructs and theories, which made perfect sense given his strong interest in Eastern spiritual thought and practice.

Before he was to leave for college, John and I had a lunch date. We went to an outdoor café that served healthy vegetarian food. (By then, he had become a vegetarian as part of his overall practice.) We were sitting across from each other when he announced to me that the next day, before he had to leave for college, he was going to visit the Brothers, hoping that he could make a decision about what he would do after college. I was sitting there eating my salad, wearing a colorful Hawaiian shirt, and all of a sudden my body became warm and I felt a strong feeling of release of all of my concerns and anxieties about the decision he was contemplating. I was able to let go and trust in him and his decisions. John did visit the Brothers to figure whether he would join them after he completed college. Wisely, the monks told him that he "could do what was important to him in life without the necessity of being a monk." By then, I was able to release him into doing whatever he needed to do in life, telling myself that each one of us is on our own chosen journey.

John has remained on a spiritual journey that began in the late seventies. A few years after he completed his BA and his master's, he got his PhD in health psychology with an emphasis on complementary and alternative approaches to health and well- being. He has kept his hand in the world of music that he loves by writing and producing a number of CDs of original contemplative music. He continues to perform his music in different venues and has developed a following.

John is a seeker, a teacher, a healer. When he was about ten years old, I gave both boys John Holland's Self-Directed Search, a test that assesses a person's career interests. John's profile indicated that he had an interest in becoming a minister. It did not make any sense to me at that time, but here he is, at fifty-four, wanting to minister to people as a healer and a teacher.

John got married in 1990, at thirty-one, and five years later had a daughter, Erin, my oldest granddaughter. Sadly, as I began writing this memoir, he divorced his wife Kat after a twenty-two-year marriage. I am hurting for all three of them. John and Kat were separated for eight months before the divorce became final. While I was not surprised when he called to tell us about it, I had believed that they had found a way of being together in spite of some fundamental differences in personalities, interests, and outlook in life, as well as in family backgrounds.

John and Kat separated in October 2012, and in November, the three of them (John, Kat, and Erin) and Paul and his family joined us in Maui during our yearly family vacation. Once when Erin, Sandy, and I were alone in the living room of our condo, we asked Erin how was she feeling about the separation. Erin is tall and striking with long, thick blonde hair almost to her waist. She said, "I'm glad it happened now instead of when I was five."

"Did you see it coming?" I asked.

"Yes and no. No, because they were not fighting. Yes, because they were distant from each other."

When John decided to leave Kat, Erin was acting in the play "Our Town," in the role of the Stage Manager. So during our conversation in Maui, she told us that the play centers on all aspects of life including what was happening in her own family and life. Seeing her parents in the audience made it hard for Erin, and she later told us that her only good performance and the only one she enjoyed was one of the matinee shows when her parents were not there. At that point, becoming emotional, I got up and hugged her hard, and the two of us cried and continued to embrace each other for a few minutes. It was a moment of a silent, strong connection. We have not spoken about the separation and the pending divorce since then. My granddaughter is a private person when it comes to her inner life and experiences.

Erin is a special young woman. She graduated in the summer of 2013 from Stevenson High School, a private college preparatory high school in Carmel, California, receiving five different honors for excellence in academic and theater performance. She is a freshman at Wesleyan University in Connecticut, where she plans to study theater and become an actor. She began to perform at age eight and had key roles in many of the various plays she took part in. Since she has a good singing voice, doing musical theater is also on her future agenda. She loves to dress fashionably, has a number of close friends, and is well-liked by teachers and other students on the Stevenson campus. In one of my early visits to her school, she took me around to show me her campus. Practically every young person we encountered on our walk around the various buildings greeted her warmly: "Hi Erin, what's up?"

– * –

I have three granddaughters who are very dear to me. Even before they reached their teens, I took them on yearly trips, some by myself and some together with Sandy. I wanted the girls to get to know us independently of their parents and outside of family trips and get-togethers. I wanted them to become close to one another. Especially, I wanted Erin, an only child, to develop a close relationship with her two cousins, Amalia and Ila, Paul's daughters.

Two years ago, the three granddaughters and I spent a magnificent long weekend in New York City. We went to the Metropolitan Museum to see the special exhibit of women's apparel through the century. What impressed them the most was the dresswear of the suffragettes followed by the sexy and playful apparel of the '20s. One of the granddaughters perceptively commented that the suffragettes dressed conservatively and in a somewhat masculine fashion: "I guess they felt they needed to do so if their concerns were to be taken seriously." I have tried to instill in them a feminist consciousness by sending them articles and editorials about feminist issues. I took Amalia to a conference on "The Status of Girls and Women in California" and to a freshman seminar at UCLA on "The Gender Gap." It is easier for me to arrange such outings with Amalia since Paul and his family live near us in Topanga, California, while John and his family have lived for years in Santa Cruz.

My most recent adventure with my three granddaughters was a ten-day trip to Paris in June 2013. A year before the trip became a reality, I was sitting with them in our family room, and one of them spontaneously said, "Grandma, next year, let's go to Paris for our annual trip."

The other two chimed in: "Yes, Grandma, let's do it. It would be perfect after Erin's graduation."

The idea appealed to me, too. To be in Paris with my three beautiful girls? It would be perfect. So without any hesitation, I said: "Let's do it."

Before I knew it, Amalia got into my computer, Googled "Home Away," and found us an apartment in the Marais district. I asked Sandy to help me find good flights. In a couple of weeks, we were all set with airline tickets and an apartment in Paris. Amalia had secured an au pair job in Paris with my goddaughter, who happens to work- as an attaché with the American Embassy. Amalia had dreamed of living in Paris, and her dream became a reality; she left for Paris two months before our scheduled departure. So before Erin, Ila, and I made our trip to Paris, Amalia had explored the city far and wide, and had become quite fluent in French, so she was able to serve as our guide while we were all together there.

What a marvelous trip! It could not have gone any better. We loved our little French apartment, enjoyed exploring the neighborhood, and visited museums, other neighborhoods, restaurants, and markets where we shopped for our groceries. We lived the Parisian life, using the Metro to get around and shopping in the neighborhood boulangerie, patisserie, fromagerie, and magasin de fruits et légumes.

Amalia had discovered a Zumba class and invited all of us to partake in it, which we did. Grandma, however, lasted only twenty minutes. Too much aerobic work for an eighty-one-year-old grandmother, exercising in a room full of young, energetic twenty-somethings.

And, as I had hoped, the girls connected affectionately. The two older ones had time alone testing their independence by visiting a bar in the neighborhood one night and going to a Comedy Store another night by Metro, while Grandma lay awake in bed, waiting for them to come back safely. I trusted them, but, I must admit, I was anxious until they got back to the apartment.

The greatest adventure and act of independence was Erin's getting a nose piercing. She had told me in advance about her plan to do so. Her mother disapproved of the idea, but felt that she could not stop her because, at eighteen, she was an adult now. She asked me what I thought of it, and I said that I agreed with her mom, that I did not think that it was a good idea, but I could not stop her from doing it. The girls Googled a tattoo parlor within walking distance from our apartment, and all four of us visited the shop to check it out. The owner, a Frenchman with lots of tattoos and piercings, was a nice man and I felt he was trustworthy. So Grandma felt okay about the whole idea. The two older girls took off the evening of the same day and came back with Erin's nose pierced. They had a positive experience with the whole process. "Amen!" A ten-day remarkable adventure in Paris ended with many memories for all four of us.

Amalia, age sixteen, fascinates me. When she was born, I looked at her and said, "She is an old soul." And in many ways she demonstrates a maturity and has insights way beyond her years. She has been homeschooled and has taken every available opportunity to expand her knowledge and skills beyond what is required of her academically. She has taken cooking lessons, sewing lessons, and has attended classes at a nearby community college since the age of fourteen. When she talks about her interest in fashion, she clarifies it by indicating that she is interested in "The history of women's fashions," and to educate herself, she checked out the appropriate books on the topic from the local library.

Ila, age thirteen, the youngest, is the artist of the group. She has been painting and drawing since early childhood. When she does her art, she focuses on it for hours, immersed in the task. Both her maternal grandmother and her mother are artists. Her grandmother is a painter and her mother is an art educator, so she has the genes for this work. But what is most impressive is her persistent love of the craft and the pleasure she gets out of it. She loves sports, running around, and playing with her friends. She is popular with her peers, who seek her out. Ila was homeschooled for a few years before she decided to attend a regular public school, where she could have her father as a teacher, an experience they both managed well.

My younger son Paul, now fifty-two, is the educator in the family. As with John, Paul wanted to earn his livelihood with his music. He managed to do so for years, perfecting his jazz piano playing, organizing a jazz quartet, and performing gigs around town. Endowed with an inquiring mind, Paul studied prehistory and anthropology in college, subjects that continue to be his passions. His knowledge of both disciplines has influenced many of his ideas about schools and education. He is passionate about teaching and about the power and importance of precollege education. His master's thesis in the fields of Latin American Studies and Public Health was a piece of action research where he taught women in a Mexican squatters settlement about nutrition. He explained nutritional principles, including how to maintain their children's health by preventing and alleviating intestinal diseases resulting from contaminated water and food in the squatter village. His teaching has always been a form of societal service, which he practices today as a classroom teacher and as an administrator. He believes in instilling this ethic of caring for others in the students he teaches, and in creating a culture of caring in the school where he serves as its principal.

Paul's love of anthropology and culture has been reflected in his love of language. He is fluent in Greek and Spanish. While John has little sense of his Greek heritage, Paul has immersed himself in Greek culture. He identifies with his Greek background and his Greek ancestors and he is the genealogist of the family. When he spent a year in Greece after college, he traveled to remote villages of central Greece to meet relatives unknown to me and to construct our family tree. He has managed to instill his love of Greece in his own two daughters. He insisted on finding the time and means to spend half a year on Paros, a Greek island, with his daughters and wife, and his family has become attached to my homeland in the same way that Paul has. I call Paul "my Greek son" and John "my American son." I have to remind John that he is half-Greek, while Paul often gets irritated with me if I do not respond to him in Greek when he converses with me in my native tongue.

For more than two decades now, I have enjoyed and valued my friendship with both of my daughters-in-law—Kat, John's former wife, and Jenny, Paul's wife. Both are strong and talented women, which I appreciate, and I have enjoyed being in their company and nurturing my friendships with them. John's divorce makes it difficult for me to know how my relationship with Kat is going to evolve, but we both want to continue our friendship and maintain our love for each other. Jenny, Paul's wife, came into my life about twenty years ago. She and Paul met at a restaurant in Venice, California, where Paul played piano and Jenny waitressed tables. It was love at first sight. In October 1991, Paul, at age thirty, wrote this in his journal, which he shared with me about three years ago:

> I met a person who interests me quite a lot. That was the real
> reason I stopped my work just now and began this journal entry. It
> is strange because, while I don't really even know who she is, I am
> immensely drawn to her being. From her first smile a week ago
> Saturday, I developed deep inner feelings for her. I continued to
> feel that way this past Saturday, and so mustered my courage to
> ask her out on a date. It seems we will get together this Friday. Her

overtly positive response to my asking her out made me feel good.
It seemed as if she might have feelings for me as well. Jenny. I've
been thinking a lot about her. She seems, from the little I've seen of
her (while playing at the Sculpture Gardens where she works) to be
a good person. Kind, creative, directed, and hard-working. Her
smile is so warm. She radiates a certain beauty that I find very
appealing on a deep spiritual level. Few people can make me feel
this way, and so quickly. How is it that I feel myself to be falling in
love when I have just met this person? I feel so good inside. I am
looking forward to getting to know this sparkling Jenny creature.

I felt honored that Paul was comfortable enough to share something like this, a private entry from his journal about Jenny. When he sent it to me, he prefaced it by saying "something romantic for my romantic mother." The entry captures Jenny. She is indeed "a very good person, kind, creative, directed, and hard-working." Jenny left home at nineteen and came to California to pursue her dream of becoming an actress. It didn't take long for her to discover that being an actor would be a harder life than she wanted, so she went to college and majored in education, while working full-time to support herself. She got her BA and a few years later, while married and with a young child, got her master's in art education. She is clearly industrious, but what makes her special is her kindness, her goodness.

The best tribute to Jenny comes from her oldest daughter Amalia: "I have the best mother in the world," she told me. And for me, I could say, without any reservations: "I have the best daughter-in-law in the world." I feel blessed to be surrounded by such a loving family.

CHAPTER 5

The '60s:
Work and Activism

In the fall of 1964, Sandy got a fantastic job offer to be the director of research for one of the major associations for higher education in Washington—the American Council on Education. The offer came with all kinds of resources and freedom to develop his own Office of Research.

We had just bought our house in Chicago, and now we had to turn around, sell it, and buy another house in D.C. And I had to find a new job. I had a good job in Chicago as a college teacher and I was respected by my colleagues, so it was hard for me to give it up. But I moved to Washington with high hopes that I would get another teaching job. And that's where, for the first time, I encountered overt gender discrimination. I applied for many college or university teaching positions, and was rejected every time. The standard reason they gave me was that I had not published, so I did not qualify. The chair of the psychology department at George

Washington University was blunt: "You finished your PhD in 1957, and now it's 1964, and you haven't published in all that time," he said. "We know from the evidence that unless you publish early in your career, there is little likelihood that you will become a scholar." I remember my reply: "Those studies were done with men, right? But women have different career trajectories." I continued, "I know how to do research. In my previous job, teaching in a small college, nobody was expected to do research. But I know I can." That didn't get me anywhere.

This kind of exchange happened more than once. Years later, I felt vindicated, given that I had published numerous books and many scholarly articles and had reached the rank of distinguished professor at UCLA.

Soon after we moved to D.C., I met one of my husband's bosses, Allan Cartter, an economist, who was the vice president of the American Council on Education. Allan was a handsome man, always impeccably dressed, with a ready smile and kind words for everyone. I liked and respected him, and trusted him to give me excellent career advice—the first time since getting my PhD that I had asked anyone. He arranged for us to meet over lunch at one of his favorite restaurants, to talk about whatever questions I had regarding career decisions. He spent over two hours with me, listening attentively to my dilemmas and numerous questions about choices and career options. I began by saying, "I really don't know what to do. I have two research job offers and also the possibility of doing some administrative work at a college. What should I do?" Without hesitation, he said that I should seriously consider one of the research opportunities. He added, "Sandy is pursuing a research agenda in the area of higher education, so I suggest that you get a research job within higher education. This way, you can get closer to his work, and it might make more sense as you guys move on. Think about long-term career objectives." I listened to him and accepted one of the research offers, that of a Research Associate for the National Commission on Human Resources in Higher Education. It was a full-time job.

Not long after I met Allan, he left the American Council on Education to become the Chancellor of New York University. In 1973, he met Jill, his second wife-to-be. Since Jill lived in Southern California, Allan left New York to be with her. In a happy coincidence, Sandy and I were at that time negotiating jobs at UCLA, so eventually all three of us came as a "package" to be professors of higher education at UCLA. Having reconnected there, Allan, Sandy, and I decided to establish the Higher Education Research Institute in Los Angeles as a nonprofit research organization. Sandy was the president and Allan and I were the vice-presidents.

Allan and I had the pleasure of preparing a course on education and work, which we team-taught. My interest in careers, his in labor economics, and our mutual interests in higher education blended well in designing and offering this graduate-level course. He came to the first class in March 1976, dressed in a navy-blue blazer, grey trousers, with the right color tie and pocket handkerchief, looking handsome as ever, but quite thin and pale. We had a good class meeting, with lots of energy exchanged between the students and the two of us. But that was Allan's last professional appearance. He was suffering from a terrible form of cancer and died a few months later, in August 1976, at the untimely age of fifty-four.

When I joined the Commission, I was a total novice to research. I hadn't done any research other than my dissertation nearly ten years earlier. I hadn't even published the dissertation article I wrote as part of my graduation requirement for the PhD. So the first thing I did in my new job was to dig it out, polish and submit it for publication in a good journal. It got accepted right away. I felt that this was a good omen.

The research team of the Commission included two men, both sociologists, and myself. There were also twelve advisors to the Commission, all men. My job marked the first time since the boys were born that I had to be at an office every day. But I was fortunate to have an employer who was a widower, raising his children by himself, who therefore understood the pressures on professional working women with children. He said, "Lena, I don't care if you leave early or if you take off because the kids are sick, as long as you do the work...I know exactly what it is like. I took off plenty of times to go and buy them shoes and coats, or take them to the doctor." He gave me permission not to feel guilty if I had to leave early or stay home and work from there. I was able to leave most of the time by three o'clock in the afternoon and be home when the boys returned from school.

The Commission was part of the National Academy of Sciences (NAS), and all twelve men on the advisory board were eminent in their fields. Among them there were several college and university presidents and presidents of foundations. Some of them were serving in key leadership roles within the National Academy. For our meetings, we would gather in one of the boardrooms in the Academy, seated around a long mahogany table, surrounded by pictures of past members and presidents of the Academy, all of whom were men. For the first two months of meetings, the word "women" never came into the conversation. Finally, during one of our meetings, I got up enough courage to say, "It doesn't make sense to me that we're talking about talent development, but we don't talk about women as a source of talent for our country."

They all looked at me in astonishment, most likely wondering about my boldness in challenging them. Some of them said, in a patronizing way, "You know, Lena, the reason we don't talk about women is because, even if they are highly educated, they stay home and take care of their children." This didn't make sense to me, since it had not been my experience. I said, "Well, how do we know that?" They looked at me in silence. I said, "Where is the evidence?" They were stunned. "Well, we don't know, really," one man said. "We know that highly educated women are important because they transmit social and cultural capital to their children." I said, "Since we don't really know, it behooves us as a national Commission to study this question, don't you think?" They replied, "Well, if you're interested, do it."

So that's how I started doing research on women and gender issues. The time was ripe: The second wave of the Women's Movement had begun; Betty Friedan's *The Feminine Mystique* had just been published; President Kennedy's Commission on the Status of Women had released its report the previous year (1963); and my own experience had sensitized me to gender discrimination. I said to myself, "Okay, they gave me permission. We have money in this Commission for studies." The first thing I thought I should do was to study highly educated and highly trained women, women with PhDs, to see what happens to them in their careers.

When I started working on this subject, I came across a book on academic women by the famous sociologist Jessie Bernard. A male sociologist had earlier written a book on academic men, so Bernard had decided to remedy the omission of women. I designed my study to look at all the women who received doctorates in 1957 and 1958, which would give me a longitudinal perspective on their lives and work-to-date. I wanted to know what had happened to them in their careers since earning their doctorates: Had they worked after receiving their PhDs, or, as the men on the Commission believed and as folklore claimed, did they stay at home raising their children? I also asked them whether they had ever felt discriminated against in the labor market.

Experiences of discrimination turned out to be paramount in these women's professional lives. But the critical finding was that the perception that highly educated women do not work turned out to be a myth. The data actually proved the opposite—most of the highly educated women in my study had entered the labor market and stayed there. Only 10% of them had left the labor market, but only for a short time, usually less than a year and a half (fourteen months, to be exact), when they had their children. My first book, *The Woman Doctorate in America*, published in 1969, was based on this study.

The book has become a citation classic. It is cited extensively by other authors because of the impact of its findings; the book's revelations had important policy implications. The chair of the Commission, Dael Wolfle, a psychologist who was at that time Executive Officer of the American Association for the Advancement of Science (AAAS), was particularly impressed. He was a prominent booster of my work, and indeed became my "silent mentor," opening many doors for me, often without my knowing. Whenever he was asked for names of people to serve on committees, commissions, and other national groups, he would always give my name.

One day I received a letter to serve on a Science Education Commission of AAAS. I went to Sandy and said, "They must have made a mistake. This must have been meant for you." In spite of my book's success, apparently I had internalized the stereotypes about women not being good enough to serve on important committees. Sandy looked at the letter and said, "I don't think this has anything to do with me." I realized that the invitation *was* meant for me, and it finally dawned on me that my work with the Commission on Human Resources and my research and publications had something to do with that. I felt embarrassed and mad at myself for assuming that women did not deserve the same status and recognition as men, and accepted the invitation promptly. I was, once again, the only woman on this new Commission on Science Education, and whenever I walked in the room for a meeting, all the men stood up and pulled out a chair for me. In those days, men felt that this was the gentlemanly thing to do, but feminists were beginning to argue that this "courtesy" was another form of inequality, because it stemmed from seeing women as "helpless." I began opening doors for men and women alike—whenever someone of either gender needed help.

The two years with the Commission on Human Resources were pivotal for my career as a researcher and scholar and as a proponent of women's rights. My sociologist colleague Alan Bayer and I published an article in *Science* on gender equity in academic employment and the reward structure in academe; our article was used by many other scholars in studies of sex discrimination in employment. Those studies collectively, and the findings reported in *The Woman Doctorate*, were critical in affirmative action legislation and in adjudicating discrimination cases.

By the late sixties, women had become outspoken about what was happening in education and in the labor market with respect to gender discrimination. The pioneers of the women's movement were becoming more visible. Women were organizing consciousness-raising groups and working on women's issues inside and outside of academia. Many of the women who were prominent in the early years of the women's movement had their training and had learned their tactics by being involved in the civil rights movement. Many had marched for civil rights. I did not as yet have direct experience with such activism; my contribution to the cause up to that time had been through my scholarly work. Research, writing, and a growing awareness of issues articulated by the women's movement were the deciding forces in developing my own feminist identity and my commitment to continue doing research and writing on issues concerning women.

The early activism of women on behalf of women and social justice had tremendous consequences, personal and political. Professional women became active within their own professional organizations, seeking to improve the status of women in their fields. In 1969, a group of women psychologists started the Association for Women in Psychology, and they marched at the meeting of the annual convention of the American Psychological Association (APA). They shut down the employment office at the convention, protesting the advertisements for jobs in psychology that indicated "men preferred." They also presented the leadership of APA with fifty-two demands. The APA accepted two of them: one to appoint a task force to study the status of women in psychology, and the second to provide child care services at the annual meetings.

In 1970, the leadership of the APA asked me to chair that task force, which consisted of nine or ten members, including four men. Our charge was to do a study of how women were faring within the association, but we decided that we were also going to be an activist group. We met with chairs of psychology departments around the country, inquiring about how they were treating women in their education and training programs and in assignments of internships. We also asked if they were offering courses in women's studies. Subsequently, we insisted that the APA appoint a standing committee that would be concerned with issues facing women in psychology. They agreed, and that committee continues to this day.

The American Psychological Association is organized into a number of Divisions (now called Societies) that represent major areas of study and research within the field. The task force, in collaboration with other APA members, helped create the Division of the Psychology of Women. To do that, we put a call all over the country for interested psychologists to come to D.C., to the APA headquarters, for the purpose of drafting the bylaws for such a Division and obtaining the needed signatures of members who were willing to support it. A group of women showed up at APA, paying out of their own pockets to get there. We met and drafted the bylaws. We collected the needed signatures and the Division was established. I was asked to serve as the first president of the Division. One of the first things we did was create a journal, *Psychology of Women Quarterly*. We made many visits to publishers and were repeatedly turned down. They regarded a journal of research on women as an ephemeral thing. "Women studies?" they said. "What's that? Psychology of women? What's that?" The journal became a reality, however, and remains the major scholarly journal on women within the field of psychology.

In 1973, Alice Rossi, a highly regarded sociologist, edited a volume on academic women titled *Academic Women on the Move*. She and her co-editor, Ann Calderwood, identified scholars around the country who were engaged in feminist scholarship and asked them to write chapters for the volume. I contributed two chapters, one of which, "Sex Discrimination among Teaching Faculty" was coauthored with Alan Bayer. He was the only male author represented in the volume. I purposely wanted to include Alan as a statement that academic men are also interested in issues of sex discrimination in the workplace.

During the preparation of the book, we discussed how our work was going to be received, and whether it would be taken seriously. We also debated how to present our names: should we reveal our full identity by using our first (women's) names or use first-name initials, on the grounds that readers would be less likely to dismiss our writing if they did not know we were women? I was alone in saying *no* to the idea of first name initials. I said, "No, we're going to have our full names and we'll do great work and I would like everybody to know that women can do excellent empirical research and scholarship…That's a statement we have to make, not disguise ourselves in order to be accepted." Finally, we did decide to go with our full first names.

During these years of my emerging feminist activism, Sandy never wavered in supporting me. I don't remember that he ever said "no" when it came to my passions. I think that his strong support for my work and our mutual respect have made it possible for the two of us to work so well together over the years. I never have felt any competitiveness between the two us, or any jealousy from Sandy about any of my achievements. But again, he had nothing to be jealous of because he already had reached the highest levels of achievement himself by the time I came into my own.

When we came to UCLA, in 1973, my kids, both in junior high school, were curious about what our salaries were. For these two teenagers, success was measured by how much money one makes. I told them that Sandy was making more money than I was. When they asked why, I said because he wrote more books than I did. Their response was "Yeah, but you had the two of us." I said, "From the mouths of babes. Go say that to the committee here—our mom deserves more money because she gave birth to two children!" I had misjudged their commercial interest in our salaries. To them, my having raised a family had a great deal of value.

As the decade of the nineteen-sixties was coming to an end and the issues of the women's movement became more visible, Sandy and I began to talk about how to divide the labor within our household and how to decide the best ways to pursue our careers so we could both feel good about our professional decisions. The turning point occurred when we were still in Washington. I learned I was being considered for the presidency of Wellesley College in Massachusetts when, as part of Wellesley's search, they wrote to Sandy's boss at the American Council on Education, Logan Wilson, for a confidential reference. Logan asked Sandy for his "permission" in recommending me for such a position. Sandy reflected on it, and replied that he was perfectly comfortable about my being considered for this prestigious position, adding that he had no problem following me there. This realization was a first for both of us, and it liberated me to go after jobs that interested me, wherever they might be—because Sandy was willing to accommodate my next choice of what to do and where to go. Ultimately, I was not offered the presidency of Wellesley College, but my career was on an upswing and other opportunities awaited.

With the boys in front
of our house in
Evanston, I.L., 1964

With Sandy in
Washington, D.C.,
just before leaving
for California,
1973

Professor Lena at
UCLA graduation,
1975

With Sandy,
Los Angeles,
1979

With Uncle Elie in Paris, 1981

At age sixty, in
California, 1992

With cousin Ioanna cruising around Cape Horn, 2008

With Sandy, Mother's Day, Topanga, C.A., 2010

With Sandy at
daughter-in-law
Jenny's art show
of her students,
2011

Sons Paul (age 51) and John (age 53), 2012

Sandy and the boys in Maui, 2012

Eighty-first birthday celebration with the boys

Sandy's 80th birthday party. Listening to a jazz performance at home, 2012

With Jenny (Paul's wife) celebrating Mother's Day, 2012

Granddaughters on a Paris holiday with grandma, Spring 2013

Visiting Alex for his 85th birthday, Pittsburgh, P.A., 2013

CHAPTER 6

An Evolving Career

In 1967, Sandy was invited to be a fellow at the Center for Advanced Study in the Behavioral Sciences in Palo Alto, California. It is an honor you do not turn down. The time was also good for me since I had just completed my work with the Commission on Human Resources and it was a perfect time to work on *The Woman Doctorate in America*, rather than having to look around for a new job. Spending a year in California also had a lot of appeal.

In the summer of 1967, we moved to Palo Alto, including Jacki, our au pair. We found a great house to rent for the year, right on the Stanford campus. It belonged to a professor who had left for a sabbatical in another state. The house was on a cul-de-sac, a modern, typical California house with many windows and light. It also had an indoor swimming pool, a dream for our boys and us, the adults, as well.

As soon as we settled, moving into the house with just our suitcases, some books, and the data for my book, I needed to find a place to affiliate with where I could write. I called Joseph Katz, one of the directors of the Institute for the Study of Human Problems. The Institute was founded by a noted psychologist, Nevitt Sanford, who was a professor at Stanford. Dr. Katz did not know me, but I told him that I needed a place where I could work on my book while getting involved with whatever research was being conducted. Before even meeting me, he said, "We would love to have you; we will give you an office, secretarial help, and some resources in exchange for your participation in a project we are just beginning about adult women's development." My research background and my interest in women's development, he said, would be a perfect match with their interests. We agreed to meet for lunch, and the deal was made.

I immediately felt close to Dr. Katz, who became a close male friend for many years, and the time I spent at the Institute was one of the most pleasant years of my career. The Institute was housed in a small two-floor Spanish house right on the Stanford campus. They gave me a beautiful office, large, nicely decorated, with a mahogany desk, a couple of comfortable armchairs, and a side table in the middle of the room. There was a large oriental rug with vibrant red and blue colors covering the dark wooden floor between the desk and the armchairs. The windows opened onto a courtyard, and in front of my window was an olive tree. An omen—I was back home in Greece! The California weather and the olive tree were symbols of my beloved homeland. My office also faced the boys' school, Stanford Elementary. John and Paul had arranged to whistle to me whenever they were out in the playground. We connected through their secret whistling.

During my year at Stanford, I completed *The Woman Doctorate in America*. I also wrote a small grant to do a monograph on women's career development, which I started while there and completed when I returned back to D.C. I participated in the Institute's Study of Adult

Women, avoiding the solitary experience of being closed up in my office writing a book. I loved the group I worked with and learned a lot from them.

Before long, I met Carole Leland, a sociologist who became one of my closest friends and has remained so. We collaborated on two other research projects and books. My work on adult women with the Institute staff prompted a later large national study I directed in the early seventies about adult women returning to education. Carole worked with me on that study and contributed one of the chapters in an edited volume resulting from it.

Thanks again to Joe Katz, I joined the College of General Education as a visiting faculty member, teaching two seminars to undergraduates. The first was "The Psychosocial Determinants of Women's Career Development." It was the first women's studies course I taught, and also one of the early courses in women's studies nationwide. (Women's studies as an academic field of study did not begin until a few years later, 1969-70.) The seminar consisted of eight undergraduate Stanford women and one man who was majoring in business. When I asked what prompted him to take the seminar, he said, "I want to understand women." Good enough reason, I thought. He was an energetic participant and a helpful contributor to the seminar.

Six years later, long after we had returned to Washington from our year at Stanford, I got a phone call from a young woman lawyer in San Francisco. "Are you the same Helen Astin who taught the seminar at Stanford?" she asked. I said, "Yes, and who are you?" She told me her name and that she had taken my seminar, which had had a strong impact on her. After Stanford, she had gone to law school and later opened a law practice, "Equal Rights Advocates," in San Francisco, which represented women who had experienced gender discrimination. She called me because they were representing a woman professor who was suing her university for sex discrimination. My former student needed an expert witness and, knowing my work, she asked if I would help them with their case. I agreed.

Being an expert witness in a sex discrimination case was my first and last experience with the legal world. The woman who sued her university had been denied the renewal of her contract because they wanted to get rid of her husband, and the only way they felt they could do that was by not renewing her contract. She had excellent credentials and was liked and respected in her field. I gave my testimony as their expert witness. The judge was interested and attentive while I spoke, but he dismissed the case for "insufficient evidence." I was devastated. I had gotten so involved emotionally with the case that I decided I would not ever serve as an expert witness again, and I haven't. I don't have what it takes to remain unattached and distant enough during court proceedings and their outcomes.

Another student from that Stanford seminar reappeared later as well—during my first faculty meeting in the department of education at UCLA in 1973. The new faculty were being introduced. She was a newly minted PhD in psychology and I was a seasoned full professor. We immediately realized that five years earlier we had been together in a different room, at a different university, in two different roles— student and teacher—and now we were colleagues at UCLA. I felt such pride to have had the chance to mentor her, for a short time, while she was an undergraduate at Stanford. She had done a creative piece of research for her class assignment, and her paper proved useful in my later work and writing for a theoretical piece I wrote on women's career development. She wanted to find out how nursery school children develop their concepts of work and careers, and she learned that work concepts have their origins in children's play activities. And since children's play activities are gender related, no wonder that such bifurcation develops early on about what is appropriate work for women and men.

While at Stanford, Sandy and I became regular faculty guests at Serra House, one of the residential halls on campus. Serra, like other houses, was a theme house; its theme was community service at a nearby enclave of Latino families in Mountain View. Each student at Serra was tutoring students in the Mountain View community. One day, a group approached me and asked if I was willing to offer a seminar on the higher education of Mexican-American students. Such a course would be one of the first offerings in Ethnic Studies.

I agreed, and because there was so little research on the topic at the time, I suggested that we as a group could do a study on the topic. The American Institute of Research (AIR) had its headquarters in Palo Alto. It was a research enterprise involved in "Project Talent," a major national study of American youth. They were collecting data on the educational aspirations, progress, and attainment of high school and college youth. I thought that that could be a resource for us to study the Mexican-American students in their sample. I asked my colleague, psychologist Lyle Schoenfeldt, who was a research associate at AIR, whether they would let us use the data to do a study on Mexican Americans. He was fascinated by the idea and generously gave us access to the data at no cost. In those days, surveys did not ask participants to provide their ethnic or racial identity, so we used the last name and location of birth to identify a sample of students that were likely to be of Mexican-American background. The eight students in the seminar and I did the study together.

Lyle Schoenfeldt was so impressed with the work the students had done that he invited us to his home for dinner to celebrate the release of our paper based on the Project Talent data. It was a warm, celebratory event. The students were grateful for his offer of data and a dinner celebration, and made a counteroffer to him and his family. The students told the Schoenfeldts they would be available to babysit their children for free at any time and as often as they needed help. It was a wonderful example of community and reciprocity.

We returned to Washington a year later, at the end of summer 1968, after a two- week vacation in the Hawaiian Islands. That trip to Hawaii generated an abiding love for the islands, so much so that we continue to vacation there yearly.

The California style of living and the pool in the Stanford house had been so pleasant that one of the first things we did after returning to Washington was to build a pool in our backyard. Since this was the only pool in the neighborhood, it became a great attraction not only for our sons' friends, but also for our adult friends, who, more than once, jumped into the pool, dress clothes and all, during party time. We became known for our parties. There was plenty of alcohol and good food, good music, and the pool to boot. You only needed one person to jump in fully dressed, and the rest followed.

Without much difficulty, I secured a position in D.C. as a research associate at the Bureau of Social Science Research (BSSR), a private, nonprofit research organization. I remained with the Bureau for two years, doing research on issues pertaining to higher education. My major effort was a study of student unrest. The years 1966-1971 were times of turmoil in American higher education. Students were protesting on their campuses against governmental policies with a focus on the Vietnam War and racial inequality, as well as their university's administrative policies and practices. At the invitation of the National Institute of Mental Health, and under the sponsorship of The American Council on Education, Sandy prepared a proposal for a national study of campus unrest. The proposal was funded and he invited BSSR and me, including my research team, to become collaborators in the study. Sandy's Office of Research at ACE assumed major responsibility for doing the national student and faculty surveys, and I and my team were to do case studies of student protests at twenty-two colleges and university campuses.

Those were exciting times. We were studying a controversial subject about controversy on campus. Some radical students attacked the study, seeing it as an instrument of the establishment that was out to get information on radical students that could be used by the government for retaliation purposes. One of the radical graduate students at BSSR who served as a research assistant notified the headquarters of the Students for a Democratic Society (SDS) about the study, asking them to notify all member campuses about it, and suggesting that they boycott the study by advising students not to participate. On some of the campuses, interviewers were sequestered and could not complete their data collection efforts. But in spite of these difficulties, the study was completed successfully, and with two other colleagues Sandy and I wrote and published our first book together, *The Power of Protest*.

That book was our first collaboration. Over the years, Sandy and I collaborated on other research projects, books, and monographs. We always had other collaborators as well, but with one exception Sandy and I took the lead role on the research projects and in the writing that resulted from the research. In all, we have worked together on seven research projects that led to published books or monographs.

Our style of collaboration is easy, because we complement each other well. I take on most of the administrative responsibilities, and, being more of a person-oriented researcher, I tend to get more involved with the interviewing part of the data collection. For his part, Sandy is a wizard with the research design and analysis parts. As to the writing, we assign chapters to each other and to others who collaborate with us. We read each other's chapters, we comment, correct, add, and discuss. It sounds smoother than it is—we also have plenty of arguments and disagreements about the work. We raise our voices, which often upsets our graduate research assistants, who tell us that our arguments have gotten them upset, "seeing the parents [us] argue and fight."

My career was flourishing. I continued to do research, write, and publish on gender issues while I was also developing my reputation as a scholar on other issues in higher education. With the completion of the campus unrest project, I left the Bureau of Social Science Research and moved on to the University Research Corporation (URC), another research and action organization. Hy Frankel, a sociologist and vice president of the corporation, recruited me to be the Director of Research and Education in the Center for Human Services at the nonprofit arm of URC. He was also instrumental in helping me get a grant to study disadvantaged students in higher education. In those days, the term "disadvantaged" was used to signify minority students who were educationally disadvantaged because of their economic status and because of having attended schools with limited resources.

At URC, I developed a strong research team that produced two annotated bibliographies, *Women's Education and Careers* and *Sex Roles: A Research Bibliography*, which was funded and published by the National Institute of Mental Health. The study on disadvantaged students was designed to explore whether compensatory programs created to help underprepared students with their educational needs contributed to their completing college. The results showed that the programs were successful, findings that resulted in recommendations for helping economically and educationally disadvantaged students to succeed. This was my second book completed and published with Sandy, together with Hy Frankel.

URC bought the property of Marjorie Webster College, a defunct private college in D.C., with hopes of starting an innovative new college for students, most of whom were African Americans, who had had encounters with the law, including incarcerations primarily for petty crimes and drug addiction. The college property was a beautiful space that had served as a two-year finishing school for women. It was located in one of the nicest areas of D.C., one of the few upscale neighborhoods that had been fully integrated. Most of its residents were professional couples, including an African-American woman who served as a secretary of Housing and Urban Planning under President Carter. Hy Frankel was appointed as president of the new college and asked me to serve as the dean, while Sandy and my colleague Carole Leland became members of the Board of Trustees.

We had great dreams of educating a population for whom a higher education could turn their lives around. Hy had realized a similar dream earlier in the sixties in East St. Louis, identifying youth who were lost and spent much of their time on the streets and in pool halls. He found scholarships for them and managed to place them in colleges around the country. Some of these students were also subjects in our study of disadvantaged students. They were a success story, and were written up by a journalist in St. Louis under the title "An Experiment in Higher Education."

Unfortunately, our dream collapsed after only a few months of the college's operation. The neighbors, feeling uncomfortable about the "type" of students we were recruiting, organized, and took the corporation to court for zoning violations on the pretext that the college property was zoned only as a residential college for women. The town meetings on this issue were volatile and contentious. In one such meeting, a rabbi who lived in the community stood up, looked around the predominantly black audience, and calmly said, "I guess the problem is that you folks do not want any young black men coming here for college." There was silence in the room, since he spoke the truth.

Eventually, the corporation and the college lost its case and the making of an innovative college came to an end. The failure of this experiment was particularly hard for Hy to bear, but we were all disappointed at being denied the opportunity to try, and hopefully succeed, in such an effort.

In 1972, I was invited to consider the position of Dean of Faculty at Scripps, a private women's college in Claremont, California. After our year at Stanford, Sandy and I had decided that if we were to make another move, California was where we wanted to go, so I responded positively to the invitation. Sandy contacted a colleague at UCLA, someone he had met at the Behavioral Sciences Center. He told him that I was being recruited at Scripps, and he wondered whether there were any possibilities for him at UCLA. This was indeed a reversal of roles. I was the one being recruited and now Sandy was looking for job possibilities for himself. His inquiry with the friend started the wheels turning at UCLA.

With the revelation "We did not know that you guys were moveable," a group of faculty and administrators organized to see if they could make it possible for both of us to move to UCLA. Given the limited number of women in the faculty, the chancellor had designated a number of high-ranking positions as "appointments of opportunity." These were positions that could be filled with women who had advanced in their careers, and the Department of Education secured one of these positions for me. But they needed a second one for Sandy, since we would only come as a package. One of the senior women faculty, Rosemary Park, a former Barnard College president, and now an administrator, said, "I am going to retire in a couple of years, so why don't we borrow my faculty line for Sandy now." Her suggestion made sense to her colleagues, who invited both of us to come to UCLA for the usual interviews, talks, and other aspects of the recruitment process.

And that is how it came to pass that, at age forty-one, we were both offered positions as tenured full professors, starting in the academic year 1973–74. (The UCLA offer was a special boon since Scripps did not offer me the administrative post after all.) We were thrilled with the prospect of returning to California on a permanent basis, with academic positions at a great university. The boys, now fourteen and twelve, were excited about moving back to California and ready for a new adventure. But the added advantage was that our boys would be close to their three cousins, sons of Sandy's brother, the actor John Astin. John and his second wife, Patty Duke, lived in Westwood, not far from us, which was another plus for our moving to Los Angeles. We had family there.

CHAPTER 7

A Bump in the Marriage

It was around the late Nineteen-sixties, twelve years into our marriage. Sandy's and my work lives were moving well, with a great deal of ease and reasonable success, but our personal lives and marriage were beginning to suffer.

Sandy was traveling often to professional meetings and conferences. He was successful professionally, and attractive. There were a lot of temptations around—young professional women for whom he was a star. He loved the attention and he was vulnerable to it. His older brother John had left his wife, falling in love with a twenty-five-year-old talented, charming, well-known actress, Patty Duke. John was eighteen years older than his young lover. That affair must have looked exciting to Sandy. At the same time, I was feeling more liberated, developing my own career and my strong feminist identity and independence. I also began to travel on my own to professional and committee meetings.

When we returned to D.C. in the fall of 1968 from our year at Stanford, I noticed Sandy becoming distant from me, withdrawing emotionally and sexually. He appeared to be depressed. Worried, I suggested that he consider seeking some help from a therapist. He complied and saw someone for a few sessions, but his feelings and behavior toward me didn't change.

In 1971, we were both invited to teach at a summer institute in Colorado. I was asked to co-lead a seminar on affirmative action with a distinguished professor of law. The first day of the seminar the professor came to class all dressed up, suit and tie. I looked surprised, given the informality of dress worn by everyone else at the retreat, and asked: "What is it with the suit and tie?" "I always do that at my first day of class," he said. "I want students to know who is the authority."

This did not go over well with me. I never felt the need to intimidate my students. He and I also disagreed in class about affirmative action. His approach was that of a constitutional scholar, while mine was that of a feminist who saw great value in implementing affirmative action given all the past inequities in education and the workplace. But in spite of our personal differences, I found him attractive and challenging intellectually, so it did not take long for the two of us to connect physically—especially given that I felt lonely and rejected by Sandy, and by our lack of intimacy.

For the next year and a half, the law professor and I carried on an affair, looking for opportunities to spend as much time together as we could. He would often come by my office in the afternoon riding his motorcycle, pick me up, and the two of us would ride through Rock Creek park, stop for a drink, make love, and talk. After that, I would go home, like nothing had happened. I would fix dinner for the kids and Sandy as always, watch TV, and go to bed. In the eyes of our friends, we were the "perfect couple," the "perfect family," while living separate and secret lives. Becoming close to another man besides Sandy, a new man who found me attractive, moved me into becoming more conscious of my looks and dress. I gave up my glasses for contact lenses, and paid more attention to how I dressed. I became more flirtatious with men in general.

As our relationship progressed, the law professor became more attached to me and expected that I would leave Sandy and move in with him. Over dinner on one of our rendezvous, I told him that my interest in him was purely physical, given that Sandy had distanced himself from me sexually, and that I had no plans to leave my marriage. He became furious and ended our relationship right then. From that point on, he did not want to have anything to do with me. He felt that his ego was diminished and that I was using him. Of course, there was some truth to it: I enjoyed his attention, his lovemaking, and his intellect, and found the illicitness of the relationship exciting.

Sandy was withdrawing even further. He was silent most of the time we were together. He would play the piano for hours at a time. When I would approach him and say, "A penny for your thoughts," he would reply, "I like my fantasy life, my private thoughts." End of conversation.

It was driving me crazy. My need for further validation about my desirability as a woman intensified. I became involved with James, then president of a small Midwestern college, when we were serving together on a board. After one of the meetings, I went to my hotel to change for an evening reception. I put on a deep blue knit dress and a single piece of jewelry, a Native American squash blossom turquoise necklace. I wanted to look good and to stand out. As soon as I entered the room, James came my way and offered to get me a drink. We spent the rest of the evening talking and, as the reception was coming to an end, he offered to drive me back to my hotel. On the

way, he showed me around town, bar-hopping. I liked his spontane-
ity, the conversation, and the fun I had with him—an intellectual
Irishman, a pretty good drinker, and a great raconteur. Being ten
years older than me, he had a certain maturity and wisdom about
him that I found appealing; I also liked his willingness to risk bar-
hopping with me around his college town, where we could have run
into his students or colleagues. Thus began a relationship that lasted
over four years.

During our years together, he was a mentor as well as a lover. I
admired him and I respected his judgment. I listened to his advice.
He gave me copies of his books and he responded to things I had
written. Sometimes he was critical of what I had written, but his critical analysis always made sense. We saw each other at board meetings
four times a year for four years and on a few other occasions; when we
were apart, we carried on a long distance correspondence. He wrote
vividly and passionately, and I could not wait for his letters to arrive
at my office. Often, when I came to town for the board meetings, he
would pick me up from the airport, about an hour's drive from my
hotel, and while driving we would spend our time together in lively
conversation.

As Sandy's and my marriage continued to deteriorate and we fell
further apart, in early spring of 1976, I suggested to Sandy that we see
someone who could help us sort out what we truly needed to do about
our relationship and our lives. He agreed, and we found Phil Oderberg, a couples' therapist who was recommended because of his reputation of working well with "high-achieving couples." During the first
session, he looked at us and asked, "Has either of you had an extra-
marital affair?"

Readily and comfortably, I said, "Yes."

Sandy's face dropped. He was shocked. He had never expected
that I was capable of such a thing, he told me later.

We worked hard in therapy for about a year. We had some marathon sessions with our therapist that sometimes lasted close to three hours.

I talked about my affair with James. But I also told James that Sandy knew about him, and that our therapist insisted that we had to give up our affairs if we were going to continue in therapy. And so I ended the affair and agreed to only see James periodically, as a friend. He understood, and we used to kid each other that, in our eighties and nineties, we would still be meeting from time to time just for a drink and a good conversation.

It wasn't to be. The friendship dissipated and we lost track of each other until, a few years later, a close friend sent me a shocking newspaper obituary describing his death by suicide. He had spent the evening before his death with two close male friends, enjoying their company and giving no indication that anything was wrong. The next morning, he was found dead in his hotel room from self-inflicted gun wounds.

To this day, when I think of him I feel a sadness, wondering what had precipitated his untimely and violent death. Was he terminally ill? Did he suffer from clinical depression? I wished that I could get some answers. And I wished that I had maintained my contact with him and had not heard about his death by reading about it in a newspaper obituary. A few months after his death, I took a brown envelope with all his letters and the obit, and threw it away. I am now sorry that I did this, but at that time it was a way of closing that chapter in my life.

During our year in therapy, my relationship with Sandy worsened. There was a lot of tension between us. I was desperately in love with him while he was fantasizing about how he was going to leave me. We fought often. I cried a lot. One evening in Malibu, we decided to catch dinner at Alice's restaurant. We were sitting across from each other. I was looking for reassurance from Sandy that we could work through these tough times and reconnect, but the only thing I could get out of Sandy was silence. In desperation, I picked up my drink of Jack Daniels with two ice cubes, threw it at his face, and stormed out of the restaurant. I could not care less if there was anyone in the restaurant who might have known us. I was hurt. I had lost all concern about decorum.

For our twentieth wedding anniversary, February 1976, I decided to give Sandy a new wedding band, as a symbol of hope and renewal of our marriage. I went to our favorite jeweler, an artisan whose work we both liked, and ordered a handmade wedding band. I told the jeweler: "It is our twentieth wedding anniversary."

He smiled whimsically and said, "Governor Brown should give you one for lasting twenty years in this town." I laughed, half-heartedly.

Our sons never asked us about what was happening in our marriage. I am sure they had to know that we were having "trouble," but they did not want to know any of the painful details. On our anniversary they presented us with a plaque, inscribed:

For Mom and Dad on their 20th wedding anniversary.

With love, John and Paul.
FEBRUARY 11, 1976

Sandy still wanted out of the marriage. He was talking of separation. As with previous times, my guardian angel made her appearance again. During the peak year of our troubled marriage (1976), I was invited to spend the next academic year (1977-1978) as the Nancy Duke Lewis Professor at Brown University in Providence, Rhode Island—a prestigious endowed chair for women who do research on gender. Without hesitation, I accepted. It felt like a perfect solution.

Sandy could have his separation from me, and I could have a professional opportunity at a highly regarded university while sorting out what could be next for us and our relationship. John was going to be out of the house, attending Berkeley. At sixteen, Paul was about to start his junior year in high school. Paul wanted to go to Providence with me, and asked me about once a day to take him along. At first, I said no. "I need my own separate time," I told him. "I need a new experience, just by myself, alone."

"I do, too. I want also to have a new experience," he said.

"If you stop bugging me, I will think and decide about it," I said.

Paul stopped asking me, and finally, I said it would be all right for him to come with me to Brown. We found a small private high school, the Wheeler School. It had started as a girls' school and had only recently become coeducational. Paul was pleased to learn that he was going to be one of only four boys in his junior year grade at Wheeler.

Brown University had given me the office of a psychology professor who was spending a sabbatical year in Denver. The professor called and asked me if I wanted to stay at their house while they were gone, as their guest, free of rent. I accepted, and Paul and I ended up living in a beautiful turn-of-the-century house within walking distance from both Paul's school and the Brown campus. I negotiated with Brown to give two or three lectures during the first semester and move to Providence after Christmas for the second semester. Paul and Sandy drove my little Scirocco car across the country, and I flew to our new home and new university.

I walked into the house, which was warmly decorated with a cozy family room and a fireplace awaiting us. I went upstairs to check the study, and what did I encounter but a map of Salonica, the very place where I had grown up during the war years. I wondered, what was a map of Salonica doing in an American home? I learned that the father of the house's owner had been one of the presidents of Anatolia college, the American college in Salonica, where I had gone to get certified for my English language competence prior to coming to the States. I went downstairs, full of emotion, and grateful to live in that house for the six months I would be at Brown. In the living room, I was greeted by Greek icons and Greek vases.

While Paul and I were in Providence, Sandy continued to see our therapist, which helped him sort out his feelings toward me and decide whether the marriage was going to survive our separation. Paul and I grew closer. He decided his role was to be there for me and to take care of me. He was the man of the house, lighting the fireplace, helping me to serve friends and colleagues some drinks or supper when they came by for a visit. He thrived. Moving from a public school with hundreds of students to one with less than forty students in his grade was beneficial academically and personally. The students at Wheeler enjoyed having a blond, blue-eyed, typical California-looking kid as one of their classmates.

I was thriving too, professionally and personally. I was appointed professor of Psychology and Sociology, and all I had to do was teach two seminars in my area of research and academic interests. I developed a couple of women's studies seminars and became involved with the Pembroke Center for Teaching and Research on Women. I joined a research study on "Women and Men at Brown University" directed by my friend Carole Leland. I also arranged a mini-university conference on the status of women, sponsored and funded by the then-president, Howard Swearer.

On a personal level, I began to feel a strong, liberating sense of independence, which meant that the possible marital separation from Sandy was not as threatening or as upsetting as it had been. I felt that I could manage fine as a separated and eventually divorced woman if that was what Sandy wanted.

Sandy wrote frequently. I kept all of his letters, which is unlike me since I tend to throw away things whenever I get into a cleaning mood. He reflected on what he thought went wrong in our marriage: "... I tended to blame you for much of the problems I saw in our early marriage, and this just locked me into the situation—put me in a frame of mind where there was no way out because it was beyond my control."

With each letter, he became more loving and expressive. He was courting me, all over again. After one of his visits to see me, he wrote: "I really loved being with you...I wanted to be with you and to understand how you felt...I was very focused on you and not feeling sorry for myself because everything was not perfect...I think I'm finding it more and more easy to be myself completely when I'm with you. I hope you do, too, because that's what love is really all about. I love you, babe."

And he continued to write: "It's such a beautiful day sitting out in the backyard today. These are the times I really miss you...When we shared these beautiful days and had lunch and wine and (sometimes!) worked. Love you, babe." In still another letter, Sandy wrote, "...It makes me feel good that you care about how I feel, whether I'm happy...I like the idea that you want to make me happy...I want you to have that power over me...To care about how I feel. Love, love, love Sandy."

When he came to visit, Sandy was affectionate and eager to be in my company. We took a short holiday to St. Croix, where he bought me a gold Florentine cross as a memento of our reunion. In return, I took a chain from my neck and put it on his. That chain has remained on Sandy's neck ever since.

After Paul and I returned to L.A., in the summer of 1978, Sandy and I had a few more sessions of therapy and we decided to make a go of our marriage. One afternoon, I turned to him and said: "Sandy, do you know that you and I could have split for good and gone our separate ways, making separate lives?" He said, "Yes, but we would have remarried each other."

The "romantic" Sandy could not have envisioned his future without me as his life's partner. But for me, getting back to feeling safe and certain that Sandy was not going to abandon me once again took some time. I felt protective of my feelings, not wanting to experience the pain I had felt in the past.

More than two decades later, in 2008, we were vacationing in Maui. Shortly after Sandy went into the water, he came out distraught. The special wedding band I gave him in 1976 had slipped off his finger, lost forever in the Maui waters. Several people on the beach dived for it, but to no avail. Ten days passed. As our vacation was ending and we were sipping our cappuccinos while waiting to leave for the airport, we noticed a dripping-wet woman with goggles and snorkeling equipment who was showing the couple sitting next to us a ring she had just found in the ocean. My heart started to pound fast. I went to their table. It was not Sandy's ring. I told her that my husband had lost his wedding ring ten days earlier.

"I'll go find it. Don't leave yet," she said, and ran down to the ocean.

Sandy and I looked at each other, and chimed in unison:

"Oh yeah, she will find it *now*?"

A few minutes later, just as we stood up to leave, she ran toward us.

"Don't leave! I found it."

And indeed, she had found the ring—in deep waters on the rocks by the sea turtles. She had found the ring, the symbol of a marriage that was destined to survive and flourish, in spite of the bumps in its way.

I am grateful to our therapist Phil Oderberg, who, over the years, has become a close friend. I am also grateful that we did not give up on our marriage, a marriage that has not always been easy, but has always had lots of love, caring, understanding, and fun times. Today, all these many years later, we still love to travel, listen to our favorite jazz as we sit next to each other silently, holding hands, in our Shan-gri-la, our beach house in Malibu.

CHAPTER 8

California and Academic Life

Los Angeles has been the city where I have lived the longest part of my entire life–forty years as of this writing. Sandy and the boys moved to L.A. in the summer of 1973, while I was still in D.C. finishing up some work, and I joined them in the fall of that same year. Before we moved, Sandy had flown to L.A. several times to do some house hunting around the neighborhoods near UCLA, our new employer. I joined him for one weekend in the late spring of 1973 to look together for housing. I knew nothing about Los Angeles or any of its neighborhoods. Sandy, the real estate agent, and I drove around the UCLA neighborhoods.

We drove up from Sunset Boulevard in Brentwood through a steep winding road to the top, a street before the uninhabited Santa Monica Mountains, to see a model house in the development. Still not landscaped, a contemporary design, with the back of the house all glassed, facing the city and part of the Pacific Ocean—a typical California house, with a fantastic view, sitting up high on a hill at 1,200 feet. It had a perfect layout and number of rooms: three bedrooms for the four of us, and two extra rooms that could serve as our studies. I did not have enough information upon which to make a decision; no idea about the neighborhood or the schools. I walked outside the house where two youngsters about our boys' ages were riding their bikes. I stopped them and asked, "How do you guys like living up here?"

In unison, they said, "We love it."

I turned to Sandy and said, " I guess this is it. We are buying this house." And we did.

I flew back to D.C. that evening, still not completely clear about the layout of the house, or whether there was room for the refrigerator in the kitchen or whether there was a laundry room in the house, and by the way, how big was the basement? I called Sandy in something of a panic about the fast decision we had made. The next day, Sandy checked with the real estate agent and called me back: "Yes, there is a space for the refrigerator, which we will need to buy. The washing machine and dryer will fit in the garage. There are no basements in L.A. houses."

Sandy and the boys moved into the house in late summer, and in November, I joined them in our new home, neighborhood, UCLA, and life in California.

After Christmas, I began a new life as an academic at a large research university. Even though I had been working for fourteen years, of which four were spent teaching at a small college, UCLA was different because of its size, its strong research orientation, its overall reputation, and its academic culture. Our appointments were in a graduate program in higher education, which meant I would be teaching a different group of students from the future schoolteachers I had taught in the early sixties at the National College of Education.

There was so much to do and to adjust to. Getting to know the area, helping the boys settle into their new school, finding music teachers for them, and, most of all, transitioning into a new and highly demanding job.

The boys, now fourteen and twelve, adjusted easily. The California weather, the neighborhood, and the public schools, worked well for them. Being an Aquarius, a water person, I wanted a pool in our new house, and we built one quickly. As they were growing up, the boys and their friends spent many hours swimming and frolicking in that pool, and I swam in it often in the summers. Our house was perched at the top of a long steep hill, but the boys learned fast to ride their bikes down, park them at a classmate's house, and walk or take the bus to school. We, in turn, would pick them and their bikes up from the friend's house on the way back from UCLA. By spring, we were getting into the swing of things and the California lifestyle. We loved living near the ocean, and being up in the Santa Monica Mountains. We loved becoming Angelenos.

Sandy and I have always had a special attachment to the sea and fond memories of it as young children and adolescents. As a child, Sandy vacationed almost every summer near the Chesapeake Bay in Maryland, and I lived by the sea, growing up in Salonica. In spring 1974, we started looking for a beach house, and the real estate agent took us to one in Malibu. We had never heard of Malibu, with all its beauty and glamour. All we saw when we arrived was a small but adequate two-bedroom house on stilts right on the beach facing the water and the historic Malibu pier. It was one of those beautiful, clear, sunny California days. The agent opened the door to the house and we saw the ocean stretched in front of the wall-to-wall glass windows. The price was reasonable and we signed the papers on the spot.

We immediately bought the essential furniture, and as soon as escrow closed, we spent our first night in our Malibu house. Paul went fishing by the pier and brought back enough fish for that first meal. Ever since, we go to our beach house every weekend and sometimes during the week as well. It takes only half an hour to get there from our main house. The minute we near the water, I get a huge smile on my face and I remind myself of how grateful I am to live here. The edge of the ocean is about thirty feet from our house, but during big storms, the waves can go under the house. In the distance at night, we can see the lights of Santa Monica, sparkling in a semicircle—a view named "The Queen's Necklace." The house is near the Malibu Lagoon, a state park with a bird sanctuary, so we are constantly visited by a parade of pelicans and other birds flying in formation over our heads and often diving into the ocean in front of our house for their fish. To our right is Surfrider's Beach, one of California's best surfing beaches, almost always full of surfers from dawn to dusk, and the location of many surfing contests.

For many years, I swam in the ocean right in front of the Malibu house, but a few years ago I stopped because the water is sometimes polluted. During the summer months, I still swim regularly in the pool at the main house.

Los Angeles reminds me a great deal of my homeland, not only because it is surrounded by water, but also because the California chaparral is similar to that of Greece. The weather, although warmer during the winter months, is still reminiscent of the Greek weather: sunny, crisp, with a clear blue sky. The landscape: lots of flowers, many hills, and blue water.

Our life in California has been enormously enriched by the many friends we have made here. Over the years, we have shared holidays and special events at both of our houses with friends—having dinners together, parties, and musicals. In the late nineteen-eighties, Sandy and I were visiting a nightclub where we heard a well-known jazz singer, Ruth Price. At the break, I went up to her and asked: "Do you ever sing at private parties, in people's homes?" She paused and said, "Yes, why not?" She had never received an invitation like this before. She wrote her phone number on the cover of a matchbook. For my fifty-fifth birthday party, Ruth Price and the great pianist Alan Broadbent performed for us and our friends. That wonderful evening marked the beginning of a series of musicals we have hosted at our home over the years.

A few months later, our friend Susan Cannon, and a friend of hers, Ron Resnick, Sandy and I brainstormed about starting a jazz co-op. The plan was to hire outstanding musicians who would play at our homes for an audience of jazz lovers. Friends would prepare food. The Jazz Co-op became a reality in 1991 and lasted six years. Susan coordinated the events, hiring the musicians, collecting the money, and organizing the list of attendees and the food that would be served. We had some of the country's best jazz musicians: Gerald Wiggins, John Clayton, Gary Foster, Eric Reed, Harry "Sweets" Edison, Buddy Collette, Les McCann, Roger Kellaway, Kenny Burrell, Pancho Sanchez, and many others. The Jazz Co-op became known in the jazz community, and other such salons throughout L.A. followed.

Ever since 1968, the year we spent at Stanford, we have a holiday tradition on Christmas Eve: a "Christmas Sing" at our home. Friends and their children come for an evening of traditional Christmas food and caroling with Sandy at the piano. We put up a tall Christmas tree, decorate with wreaths and candles, and the smell of food and glögg fill the house. The one year I cancelled, feeling too tired to plan and cook, our friends were so disappointed that they insisted we resume the tradition. We did, but now I cater it, the same foods every year: roasted turkey, sweet and sour meatballs, lots of cheeses, crudités, little vegetarian sandwiches, the usual glögg and many sweets. Sandy designs the invitation—"Join us for the Christmas Sing at the Astins" (no RSVP)—and sixty to seventy people come, often bringing their own friends. All ages are represented, from newborns to people in their nineties. We have seen little children of our friends grow up, get married, and now bring their own children to the party. As one friend commented, "This is 'Our Town'."

Some of our friendships have lasted as long as Sandy and I have lived our lives together. Even though some of these friends live in other parts of the country, we arrange get-togethers, including annual travels. Together, we have celebrated special birthdays and anniversaries and our children's weddings. Sandy acts as our travel agent, choosing the location and arranging all of the logistical details. I am writing this just as we returned from a week in the Canadian Rockies with two couples who represent a friendship of fifty-seven years. Five of the six of us are in our eighties. Walking is getting harder; canes are essential for two of us, and we need to stop for a rest more often than we did. And while the Rockies were a feast for the eyes—providing breathtaking views of mountains, lakes, glaciers, endless rows of pines, and majestic waterfalls—the sweetness of the friendship over all these years is what warms the heart and replenishes the spirit.

Life at UCLA

As soon as I arrived at UCLA, the executive vice chancellor appointed me to a committee to advise him on whether UCLA should establish a women's studies program. I had promised myself that I would always make sure to serve on a committee or task force that would be concerned with the status of women on campus. The committee consisted entirely of senior women faculty known for scholarly accomplishments in their disciplines, but not necessarily known for their feminism or scholarship on gender. I was the only one on the committee who represented these interests and expertise.

I had just published an article that examined the early years of women's studies programs. The first program was inaugurated in 1969, and two years later, the International Social Science Journal commissioned me to write an article on women's studies in American colleges and universities. My then-research assistant, Allison Parelman, and I found thirteen existing programs. We examined how they got started, what courses they offered, and what issues they confronted in trying to get established. Our article, which appeared in 1973, was also translated into French.

Our committee concluded that a women's studies program should be established. However, in typical bureaucratic fashion, our recommendation was not enough. Because it was an academic program, it had to be reviewed by another committee appointed by the dean of the College of Letters and Science, given that the program would be housed in the College of Letters and Science. I was not a member of this second committee because my department was not located in the College, but I worked with them as their consultant. They echoed our recommendation, and a women's studies specialization was established in 1976. I served on and chaired the advisory committee of the program and also taught in the program.

Two more activities pertaining to women's concerns at UCLA in which I played a key role during my years at the university involved my chairing the chancellor's Affirmative Action Compliance Committee and the founding of the Center for the Study of Women.

In 1981, a group of twenty-eight scholars affiliated with women's research centers around the country met in New York City and founded the National Council for Research on Women—a coalition of centers dedicated to advancing the rights of women and girls through research, policy, and advocacy. I was part of that historic meeting. Excited and full of energy, I returned with the idea of creating a research center for the study of women at UCLA. I wrote a précis of the vision for such a center that two of my colleagues, Tama Kaplan and Karen Rowe, expanded into a full-blown proposal that Karen and I shepherded through numerous committees and meetings before the Center for the Study of Women was established as an organized research unit in 1984. It was the first such unit involving research on women and gender in the entire University of California system. Today, there are more than two hundred scholars affiliated with the Center, representing many departments throughout UCLA, and it is recognized nationally and internationally for the research it produces on women and gender.

I chaired the Advisory Board for the Center and headed the Center for two years as its interim director. My affiliation with Women's Studies and my involvement with creating and leading the CSW have been two of my most cherished experiences during my tenure at the university. The research, scholarship, and programs of the CSW have been instrumental in helping us rethink and transform the way we approach our work in the disciplines at the theoretical and methodological levels. These activities have transformed the disciplines and our teaching practices. The CSW has provided a home for feminist scholarship and created opportunities for mentoring the next generation of scholars through its programs for graduate students and a number of fellowships and other monetary opportunities made available to young scholars.

I felt it was important to have the Center be a part of the "community" beyond the campus. We co-sponsored a conference with the School of Architecture and Urban Planning titled "Learning from the South." The "South" involved two populations of women: scholars of feminist studies from South America and activist women who were leaders in their local communities, mostly Latinas and African-American women, who lived and worked in southern and eastern L.A. Some of them were members of Mothers Against Gangs, having lost their own children in gang wars. Others had organized household laborers (maids and cleaning ladies) to know their rights and fight for them. We also reached out to more affluent women outside of UCLA to become our supporters, providing financial support and fellowships for scholars and graduate students affiliated with the Center.

My activism on behalf of women at UCLA has occupied a great deal of my professional activity and service over the thirty years I have spent on the faculty. Feminist activism has been closely interwoven with my scholarly work. Almost two-thirds of my published work has dealt with issues concerning women and gender. My personal experiences, combined with being present at the onset of the second wave of the women's movement in the sixties and early seventies, fueled my own passion toward activism. I saw myself as a scholar-activist in my research, writing, and service.

My Years as an Academic Administrator

In the early eighties, UCLA's chancellor appointed a committee to assess the administrative structure of the College of Letters and Science, and to recommend a reorganization that could enable the College's administration to be more effective. The College of Letters and Science is the largest unit on campus in terms of the number of graduate and undergraduate students it serves and the size of its faculty. The College enrolls over twenty thousand undergraduates, about three thousand graduate students, and close to a thousand faculty members. When I was appointed to the reorganization committee, the College was administered by a dean and four associate deans, each serving at one of the four major divisions: Humanities, Social Sciences, Physical Sciences, and Life Sciences.

After our reorganization committee did its work, we recommended that the position of the dean convert to that of provost with greater administrative authority, and that instead of associate deans, they appoint four deans, each with their own budget. The committee also recommended the creation of a new position, that of an associate provost with major responsibilities for undergraduate education, who could initiate new programs to enhance the undergraduate experience and conduct research to assess undergraduate programs and the students' overall academic experience.

In 1983, the administration implemented the key recommendations of our committee. A new provost was appointed and a search got under way for the appointment of an associate provost. I was nominated and became its first occupant. My portfolio included all academic support services including advising, tutorials, and special programs for academically underprepared students, most of whom were students from underrepresented ethnic and racial backgrounds. The position also included the creation of an Office of Research, with some limited resources for academic initiatives for undergraduates. UCLA culture focuses its energies and resources on research and graduate education.

I felt ready for the job but the administrative culture of the College was not ready for me to be the first woman administrator in charge of a large academic unit. The provost and the four academic deans, all men, created problems. The provost was an eminent physicist, energetic, self-confident, with high aspirations about someday getting the Nobel Prize for his research on fractals. He was also immodest. He would read all the reviews of faculty who were up for promotion or new appointments and render a final decision, no matter what their area of expertise. Sometimes, he would second guess the recommendations of review committees with expertise in the candidate's special field. One day, I asked him how he could judge a professor's work in fields so different from his own, such as literature. He said, in his usual confident way: "No problem, I can see the merits of the case using my judgment."

I had different relationships with each of the deans. The Humanities dean was a wise man, with degrees in philosophy and law, and was a psychoanalyst besides. Since he lived near us, he occasionally gave me a ride to off-campus meetings and events. We had a special connection, given my psychology background and his psychoanalytic training. The dean of Life Sciences was a dynamic young man who would often bend the bureaucratic rules to assist me with some needs of my division, usually for special equipment. The Social Sciences dean was a psychologist who shared my political interests and commitment to social activism. He supported me whenever I raised issues that had to do with equity concerns. The dean of Physical Sciences was friendly but our interactions were few and far between.

My nemesis was the assistant vice provost for Budget and Finances. He had a chip on his shoulder, which I think stemmed from the fact that he was not an academic. He was competitive with me, quick to obstruct any new programs and recommendations I proposed. I believe he had hoped to be the one appointed to the post of associate provost, but, unfortunately for him, he did not come from the faculty ranks and the position of associate provost was designated as an academic administrative post.

At the end of each academic year, we prepared our budget proposals for the next year. My budget was determined directly by the chancellor, so I drafted my pitch for what I needed for undergraduate education initiatives for him. At one of our weekly meetings of the Cabinet, I was to make my preliminary budget presentation and get feedback from the provost and the deans. No one listened to me. Indeed, as I was talking, two of the deans made paper airplanes and began to throw them at each other, acting like adolescents. I was furious. I stopped my presentation, stood up, looked at them, and said: "You know, guys, what you are doing? You are doing 'gender.'" And I walked out of the room. The next morning I walked into my office, and there, awaiting me, was a beautiful arrangement of flowers with a brief note signed by the two deans: "For Lena: Mea Culpa."

The financial support I had from the provost and his financial officer (the assistant vice provost) was practically nonexistent. One of
the first programs I was interested in introducing was a Student Research Program (SRP) that enabled undergraduates to work with faculty on their research. Such programs can have a significant impact
on undergraduates, especially those attending a large research university where personal contacts with individual faculty are limited. What
programs can be created that would bring undergraduates into a closer
relationship with faculty and graduate students?

MIT had one of the earliest and best such programs in the country, so I invited its founder, a woman scientist faculty member there,
to come to UCLA to talk about their program. My advisory committee and staff members attended the seminar. We were all enthused
about such a program and ready to embark on its creation. We wrote
a proposal that I presented to the Cabinet with a request for a small
administrative budget, just enough money ($16,000) to create a bro-
chure and fliers announcing the program.

My nemesis, the college's assistant vice provost in charge of finances, shot us down. "Not a good idea at all," he said. "Why would
our faculty want to work with undergraduates when they have graduate students to use in their research? Only faculty who are 'losers' will
volunteer to work with undergraduates." I could not believe his attitude and the language he used to express his disdain.

Undeterred, I decided to forge ahead, working with Lucy Black-
mar, who served as my right hand. I had met Lucy soon after arriving
at UCLA. One of the vice chancellors had given me a small grant
($19,000) to undertake a research project that would evaluate teach-
ing effectiveness. Lucy, who is sixteen years younger than me, was
then a graduate student in the Department of Urban Planning. We
worked together for a couple of years on that project, which was the

beginning of our close colleagueship and friendship that has lasted more than forty years.

After Lucy got married and had children, she took a short time off from work. When she learned about my appointment as associate provost, she called me, wondering whether I had any part-time openings. Perfect timing, I told her; I could use someone like Lucy as an executive assistant. We were the perfect team. We dreamed together about what innovations were possible for undergraduate education, we wrote proposals, and we introduced a number of programs.

I now saw that our budget could use some of our existing resources to create the Student Research Program. Eric Goshen, an honor's undergraduate student, volunteered to help. Lucy, Eric, and I approached faculty members, asking them whether they were willing to take undergraduate students as research assistants in their research labs and projects. Ninety-one faculty members were eager and willing to offer research opportunities for undergraduates. We also identified a hundred students who were interested in working with faculty. Next, we printed a booklet that described the faculty members' research and other materials about how to apply and what was expected from both faculty and students. (Lucy's husband, an architect and designer, designed our first brochure so the only cost to us was printing.) The Student Research Program was launched during the 1985-86 academic year, the first such program among all the eight campuses of the University of California system.

After it was up and running, of course, the provost took great pride in talking about it and its success whenever he had the opportunity to do so. Today, the SRP serves more than two thousand students; a thousand faculty members are mentors of undergraduate students doing research with them. Many students end up publishing with their faculty mentor and present their work at national conferences.

Another project that Lucy and I felt especially proud of was a complicated effort to incorporate gender and ethnic perspectives into general education courses. We managed to secure a grant from the U. S. Department of Education to support the effort, which turned out to be the beginning of a major curricular transformation effort at UCLA. The University chose not to make a course on gender and/or ethnic studies a requirement, but did create opportunities for students to learn about other cultures in various general education courses. Faculty in four departments and two programs were assisted in changing their syllabi to incorporate gender and ethnic perspectives. They participated in seminars that exposed them to readings and discussions of gender and ethnic perspectives, and brought in speakers who were experts on these topics. One of my graduate students, Paula Ries, observed all of these sessions for an ethnographic dissertation she did for her PhD in higher education, an important early piece of research to document the process of curricular transformation. That project was continued with additional grants and leadership from another faculty member, Karen Rowe.

My activist work interfaced with teaching and scholarship. Teaching enabled me to create courses that dealt with feminist concerns, such as a seminar on Women in Higher Education (offered through Women's Studies and also the Department of Education, for graduate students), one on women in academia, and a third on students' development during the college years. It was designed to introduce students to developmental theories that critiqued earlier theories based solely on studies of male development.

In 1983, my friend and colleague Carole Leland and I decided to bring together a group of forty-five women from education, business, and politics to reflect on the accomplishments of the Women's Movement and outline a future feminist agenda. We got a small grant from the Ford Foundation to help support the conference. The Johnson

Foundation also assisted us by hosting the conference at the Wing-spread Center in Wisconsin, a beautiful facility built by Frank Lloyd Wright. The conference, entitled "Women of Influence, Women of Vision," was such a success that it energized Carole and me to do some further scholarly work. With additional support from the Ford Foundation and the Exxon Education Foundation, we embarked on a study of women in education, broadly defined, who had provided leadership on behalf of women during the onset and early years of the Women's Movement. We identified three generations of women: the Predecessors, who did some of the groundwork in the late nineteen-fifties and early Nineteen-sixties; the Instigators, who were the visible activists during the second part of the decade of the sixties; and the Inheritors, who were mentored by the Instigators to continue the work that they had started.

We interviewed seventy-seven women around the country repre-senting the three generations. They had been identified through a nomination process as having been instrumental in bringing about change on behalf of women. We wanted to know about their leader-ship and their work during the critical years of the second wave of the Women's Movement. The study culminated in our book *Women of Influence, Women of Vision: A Cross-Generational Study of Leadership and Social Change*. It is the personal story of these leaders and their activism for equal rights.

The Higher Education Research Institute

When we left Washington in 1973 for Los Angeles, the president and Board of the American Council in Education, where Sandy served as director of research, recommended that Sandy move his whole research enterprise to UCLA. By then, Sandy had built an ex-tensive program of research in higher education with large databases and grants to support that research. Moving to UCLA, with an established program of research, was a great advantage for us and for the students we were going to be teaching and training. Since there was no available space in the School of Education to house the program, we were encouraged to locate it off campus but near the university.

Since our friend and Sandy's former colleague, Allan Cartter, was eager to move to L.A. to be with his soon-to-be wife, Jill, the opportunity to affiliate with us at the Institute was too good to pass up. So the three of us, over a long lunch, decided to establish the Higher Education Research Institute as a nonprofit organization, and to find a space for it. Sandy became the president and Allan and I were the vice presidents. Who would have predicted that Allan, who had been one of Sandy's bosses at the American Council on Education, and a member of the National Commission where I did my first serious research in the nineteen-sixties, would end up as our colleague in our new jobs and lives at the other end of the country?

The administration at UCLA was delighted with our plans. Seeing that our data and research projects would provide a great opportunity to train graduate students, they provided a base funding of eighty thousand dollars per year to support research assistantships for graduate students. Sandy and I needed to be available to teach and do committee work, so we hired someone to serve as the executive director, to manage the Institute: Lew Solmon, a Chicago-trained economist, who had been doing cutting-edge research in higher education. Lew and Vicki, his wife, became two of our closest friends. Eventually, both Lew and Allan were appointed as professors of higher education in the same program in which Sandy and I had our appointments. The four of us ran the Institute, and did a lot of research and training there as well as teach graduate seminars and courses in the department.

Both Allan and Lew are no longer with us. Allan died suddenly from cancer at age fifty-four, just three years after we established the Institute. He had had just three beautiful years with Jill and his adopted family. UCLA subsequently established a Chair in Higher Education in Allan's name. Lew eventually became dean of the Graduate School of Education, then left UCLA to work in a private foundation. He died of a stroke in 2008, at the age of sixty-five.

The Institute's national program of research, which continues to this day, has brought great visibility to both UCLA and the School of Education. The program involves an annual national survey of entering college students' characteristics, values, beliefs, attitudes, and educational and career aspirations. Each entering class can be followed up longitudinally. Data are also collected triennially from faculty from over four hundred institutions. These sources of data and other data collected through grants from foundations and the federal government provide a gold mine of research data for many of our students.

– * –

Sandy and I retired formally in 2002. Mentally, I knew it was important for us to step down and vacate our positions to make room for new blood, but emotionally, I was not ready for retirement. I had a hard time calling myself "emerita" or telling people that I was now retired. The dean of the School of Education suggested a retirement party for us, but I declined her kind invitation. I felt I had lost my identity. I was apprehensive about how was I going to fill in my time with meaningful endeavors. I was a mess. I had anxiety dreams. In one powerful dream, I was a homeless person. And in my dream, I felt the lightness of not having a home and things to worry about and take care of, but also a deep sadness of not having the warmth of a home. I sought short-term therapy to figure out what I should do with my life.

But then Arthur Schwartz, a senior officer at the Templeton Foundation, approached Sandy and me and asked us to prepare a proposal to the Foundation for a national study of the spiritual development of college students. He came to us, he said, because we had done a number of national studies of college students through our Institute, had the data and facilities to undertake such a study, and had shown a genuine and persistent interest in the topic. We had earlier been invited by the Fetzer Institute in Kalamazoo, Michigan, to participate in a series of dialogues on "Authenticity, Wholeness, and Renewal" in higher education. Afterward, some of us, including Sandy and me, organized a steering committee to prepare a statement about the importance of spirituality in higher education, and presented within the larger higher education community a series of dialogues similar to those we had engaged in at Fetzer.

Once awarded the grant from the Templeton Foundation, we undertook a national eight-year study of the spiritual development of college students. We published the results of this study in a book written by Sandy, our colleague Jennifer Lindholm, and me, called *Cultivating the Spirit: How College Can Enhance Students' Inner Lives*. This work has provided meaningful closure for me at the end of an active and fulfilling career. From writing my dissertation on empathy to doing my last large piece of research and writing on spirituality completed a cycle that reflects my strong interest in people's inner lives, personal qualities, and beliefs.

Jessie and the Ouija Board

Over the years, Sandy has become interested in supernatural phenomena as well as the work of Jane Roberts, a channeler of a disembodied spirit named Seth. Seth's books channeled through Roberts set forth his metaphysics and philosophy, which have had a great appeal to

Sandy. As part of his search and need to understand all kinds of supernatural phenomena, Sandy came into close contact with a small circle of friends, most of whom live near La Jolla and are also interested in the Seth material. They have been meeting once or twice a year for a number of years now and to be together as often as time permits.

About four years ago, I joined Sandy on his travels south to meet with the group. I liked the way they accepted each other and the warmth and love they showed toward each other. They welcomed me instantly and I became a member of their circle. Our gatherings last a weekend. There is a structure to what takes place during our time together. Our regular host, Walter Eckhart, is a molecular biologist who served for many years as director of the cancer research program at the Salk Institute. We usually spend Friday evening at the home of Walter and his wife Karen. The two of them and a couple of other members of the group prepare a wonderful meal.

After dinner, the Ouija Board is brought out and Walter and Karen get on it. They have become adept at it. We all gather around them and call to some of our loved ones on the board. What has amazed me is that such a group, consisting mainly of highly educated people, mostly scientists, has delved into psychic phenomena, searching for the unknown, reflecting the need for exploring whether there is something there, something beyond the material—a soul, a spirit that exists after death.

One day, I ventured to call Jessie on the board. Jessie was my friend Lucy's daughter, who died at twenty-four after an unusual paralyzing illness that struck her at age sixteen, completely unexpected. On Christmas Eve of 1994, Jessie was in our house with her family for our Christmas Eve party. She and her sister Emma, two years younger, looked beautiful that night. They were dressed to the nines, going to a party after our event. The next day, Jessie flew to Montana to spend a few days of her Christmas holidays skiing with a girlfriend and her family. While she was trying to put her ski boots on, she realized that her feet and legs would not cooperate. In a panic, she called her mother, who told her that she must have been nervous not knowing how to ski, or having to take a ski lesson for the first time.

But the next morning, Jessie woke up completely paralyzed; she had a neurological disease called Neurofibromatosis Type 2. She was flown to UCLA Emergency for an extensive period of hospitalizations requiring many forms of treatment and resulting in numerous setbacks. Her health continued to deteriorate, and eventually she lost her mobility completely. Her vision and hearing were compromised. Her speech was difficult to understand. But her spirits soared. In spite of this horrible illness, Jessie completed high school and entered the University of California at Berkeley as an undergraduate student. Jessie has been my hero. Her inner strength, her exceptional talents, and her determination have been not only remarkable, but also immensely inspiring. She was one of the most talented young persons I have ever encountered. She was a painter and continued to do so even with her limited mobility. She wrote poetry and short stories. She was a straight-A student at Berkeley and a strong advocate for students with disabilities.

My friend Jessie died before her twenty-fourth birthday. She taught me many lessons of how one can live life to its fullest in spite of enormous physical disabilities. In my eulogy, I quoted Cornel West: "Hope is about struggle, making a leap of faith, because the future is still open-ended. It is that sense of struggle against the odds and against the grain." That so described Jessie. It was that hope, that faith that sustained her against the odds and against the grain. She knew the power behind life. She never lost her hope, her faith, her passion; the beauty that she loved all around her. It has been now thirteen years since her passing, and she still comes to teach and inspire me about how to live life fully and meaningfully.

When I called for Jessie to come to us through the Ouija Board, we had the following conversation:

Lena: "I would like to know what has happened to Jessie, a dear one to me."

Jessie: "Hello. Yes, you were very dear to me. This is very strange. I have not talked to anyone like this before. No one has tried to reach me. I am so happy to see you. I hope you will continue to think about me. I can see now your kind thoughts toward me are like glowing lines of light shining out to me."

Lena: "Are you happy?"

Jessie: "Yes, I am happy, but I didn't realize it until just now. I think I have been in a fog, not really knowing where I was or what I was doing. You have shined some light on me. I am very grateful...I hope you will continue to connect with me because...Look for me in a dream. Now I am fading."

Some of Jessie's ashes are spread in the waters of Leo Carillo beach in Malibu, not far from our beach house. One of my most special memories with Jessie was during a brilliant day on the deck of the Malibu house. Jessie was determined to write a proposal for a program to be offered at UCLA about students with disabilities. She wanted my assistance on how to frame it. She did draft that proposal as part of a summer course she was taking at UCLA, and the disabilities program became a reality thanks to the persistent efforts of her mother Lucy. A yearly fellowship for students in the program is named after Jessie: the Jessie Alpaugh Award.

More of the Paranormal: Spoon Bending

Besides my experience with the Ouija board, a second paranormal experience was an evening that involved spoon bending. We were attending a retreat of our spirituality group at a friend's family compound in the north woods of Wisconsin. Sandy had suggested that, as part of our retreat, we should invite a professor of engineering who had conducted a number of spoon bending events to join us. He came to our retreat with a suitcase full of spoons and forks for the demonstration. He set all twelve of us in a circle and explained how he was going to direct us through the bending exercise. He handed each one of us a utensil of our choice. I chose a teaspoon. He asked us to hold the utensil in front of our face, and with complete concentration direct the spoon or fork to bend. I was very focused. I held that spoon in front of my face, staring at it and repeating "bend, bend, bend..." When, all of a sudden, the handle of the spoon became soft as putty and with no effort whatsoever, I kept twisting it, thus ending up with a spoon handle looking like a corkscrew. A couple of other people managed to bend or twist their utensils. Sandy was frustrated and so was one of our other participants, a physicist, who continued to hold his fork and stare at it. And then, to our amazement, the outside prongs of the fork moved in different directions, sideways and up and down.

What can I say? I am still puzzled. Am I a believer? I would say that there is still a good dose of skepticism on my part about paranormal phenomena. I am fascinated by what I observed, and I do believe in the power of our minds. As the young people would say: "Go figure..."

Epilogue

I turned eighty-two on my birthday in 2014. I am in the last decade or decade and a half of my life, if I am granted this time. It is only when I think of my age that the finality of our lives and ultimate death go through my mind; otherwise, I feel vigorous and young. I had been blessed with good health until just after completing the first draft of this memoir, when I was diagnosed with pancreatic cancer. But I still feel that I have many years ahead of me, years that I can enjoy fully. My body continues to work well. I feel energetic, able to daydream about and plan the next travel adventure. Sandy and I still manage to play hard, to listen to music, visiting jazz clubs whenever we can, traveling and enjoying social gatherings with friends and family.

For the past ten years, I have taken up exercising. I go to a nearby studio twice a week for Pilates exercises. I am the oldest client there, but I would say that I measure up pretty well to all the other clients, most of whom are much younger than I am, and many of whom have beautifully tanned and strong bodies. I am amused by my own pleasure in doing Pilates, because exercising was never my favorite pastime. As a young student in Greece, whenever we had gymnastiki (exercise class) I would hide behind someone in front of me and not do any of the exercises. But, starting in my seventies, I have become an avid Pilates participant and fan of this exercise form. I keep joking with friends and my trainer about starting to do informercials about Pilates.

About thirty-five years ago, I decided to join a gym for women that had just opened in the community near where we live. I felt that it was about time for me to start doing something about my body. I paid my yearly fees and checked the group exercises for a couple of weeks. I hated the whole thing, but I quickly discovered the pleasure of massage. A young woman of twenty-seven, Carol, was a masseuse in the gym. I tried her massages once or twice and got hooked. And now, thirty-five years later, Carol continues to come to the house every Monday evening to give me my massage. Every year around tax return time, Sandy kids me that I spend quite a bit of money on my body, with my weekly massages and my Pilates lessons.

"Sandy, it is the best thing I can do for my health now, for my physical and emotional well-being. It is better and more helpful than any psychotherapy," I say. He looks at me lovingly, and every time I leave the house for my Pilates session, or for my massage next door, he says with a smile, "Have a good one." And he plays the piano for me whenever I have a massage session.

Returning Home

My beloved Greece has been very much in my mind these days. Greece's economy is suffering badly, and one senses the desperation among most of the Greeks I have spoken with in recent months. Their pensions are cut by 40 percent, the taxes have almost doubled, and the unemployment for those in their twenties has climbed to around 60 percent. In order not to go bankrupt, Greece has accepted large loans from the European Union with the promise that they will undertake stringent austerity measures. This has caused widespread unemployment and depression for many middle-class Greeks, including my relatives. Tourism has dropped, but Greece's beauty still manages to attract its loyal visitors. Sandy and I just completed our regular biannual visit there during the spring of 2014.

Our usual visit includes a stay of two to three days in Athens, where most of my remaining relatives live. Our get-togethers are joyous. We gather either at my cousin Ioanna's apartment with its huge veranda or at a nearby taverna. Ioanna prepares all the food when she hosts the gathering. It is a large spread of Greek food, usually much more food than we can possibly consume, ending with rich desserts. Stavros Taverna is the favorite for all of us. The table is set up by Stavros and his two daughters with an assortment of beautifully prepared traditional Greek food: calamarakia, horta (greens with lots of lemon and olive oil), freshly baked bread, and two to three kinds of Greek cheeses. A big bowl of horiatiki salata (tomatoes, cucumber, green peppers, feta, Kalamata olives and olive oil) sits in the middle of the table. The grilled fresh fish follows and the evening meal ends up with a huge tray full of baklava, a traditional Greek dessert. Fruit is on the proprietor.

After our visit to Athens we go to a couple of islands, spending four or five days at each. Greek island life is idyllic. Each island has its own culture with its unique architecture. The foods also are unique to each island. What the islands have in common is the Mediterranean that surrounds them and the Greek philoxenia—the love of the stranger. The islanders make you feel perfectly at home, taking good care of you, and treating you like a member of the family. There are over one hundred thirty inhabited islands in Greece, of which we have visited thirty-three so far.

— * —

On occasion, Sandy and I have talked about our wishes for how we want to be treated after our death. For a long time I would say to Sandy in seriousness, "I do not want to be buried. I can't stand the idea of going underground in a coffin. I am too claustrophobic. Also, I do not like to be burned."

"Then I would have to hang you from a tree," Sandy responds, and the conversation ends up in laughter. But I continue to think about it, and a question soon pops up in my mind: "How can I return back home at the end of my life's journey?" The only way is cremation. The family can take me back home and spread my ashes in the beautiful Aegean waters. And after that, I can see them going up to my favorite restaurant, the "Greek House," by the Acropolis, that is all lit up. The full moon lights up the whole place. The fresh evening air mixes together with the delicious smells of Greek food that is being lovingly prepared and served. The music is the soft, beautiful Greek music I so love.

The waiter brings a bottle of Greek wine and a tray with mezedakia. The glasses are lifted and my beloved family is bidding me farewell. John picks up his guitar and sings softly:

Blessings on your journey
Blessings on your way
On your way back home
Just carry the light
Within you...

"Sandy," I will say from beyond, "remember to call me on the Ouija board next time you are in La Jolla. I'll tell you all about what's happening up here. But, most of all, I'll tell you: Thank you for being my partner, my soul mate through this amazing journey. You are the best playmate, and I love you."

THANKS

My son Paul has been asking me to write my memoirs as a gift for my family and most specifically for my granddaughters. So I owe Paul a huge amount of gratitude for insisting that I take this task seriously, as a responsibility towards my family. Thank you, Paul.

Thank you, Chick, for bringing Nicky into my life and this work. Nicky has been my guiding source of inspiration in writing about my journey. She has been my teacher, my mentor. I could not wait to send her sections of my writing, anxiously looking at my emails for her response. I learned from her how to write using nonacademic prose. Her notes from Vermont inspired me to write and rewrite with pleasure. Thank you, Nicky.

And there were all of my dear friends encouraging and supporting me to do this writing. Thank you Engin, Carol, Anne, Lucy and all of my other friends who were asking me about my progress and telling me how they were anxiously awaiting the finished product. Thank you, thank you, all. But especially my dear friend Carol Tavris who became my "agent" in making sure that the memoir got published. Thank you, my friend, for taking over when I started my treatments, for editing and providing needed corrections before it went to Marco Pavia, my designer, copy editor, and producer of the memoir.

Since I am a very bad typist (one hand, one finger), I could not have done this without the assistance of Leigh Ann and Christina. Thank you both for your help. You were integral to this process, so very helpful and engaged.

Sandy, my husband and partner in this journey for 58 years, has been there for me all the way, from helping me navigate my computer to helping with editing of the manuscript. Sandy, thank you for being you, my love, over our years together.

My dear son John encouraged me and supported me in this process. John, you have been eager to learn about me, and my life. Thank you for always being there for me, calm and loving.

Memories are just what we remember. Sometimes they are very accurate and other times just pictures we carry with us of the people around us, the places we have been to, and the events that shaped us and have stayed with us; stories we have told to ourselves. Enjoy my journey as much as I have enjoyed the process of writing about it.

35165839R00119

Made in the USA
Lexington, KY
01 September 2014